Firewall Design and Analysis

SERIES IN COMPUTER AND NETWORK SECURITY

Series Editors: *Yi Pan (Georgia State Univ., USA) and*
Yang Xiao (Univ. of Alabama, USA)

Published:

COMPUTER AND NETWORK SECURITY

Vol. 4

Firewall Design and Analysis

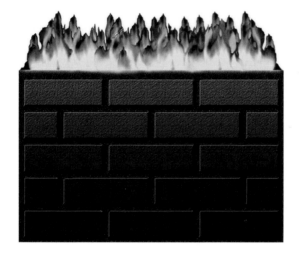

Alex X. Liu

Michigan State University, USA

World Scientific

NEW JERSEY · LONDON · SINGAPORE · BEIJING · SHANGHAI · HONG KONG · TAIPEI · CHENNAI

Published by

World Scientific Publishing Co. Pte. Ltd.

5 Toh Tuck Link, Singapore 596224

USA office: 27 Warren Street, Suite 401-402, Hackensack, NJ 07601

UK office: 57 Shelton Street, Covent Garden, London WC2H 9HE

British Library Cataloguing-in-Publication Data
A catalogue record for this book is available from the British Library.

FIREWALL DESIGN AND ANALYSIS
Computer and Network Security — Vol. 4

Desk Editor: Tjan Kwang Wei

ISBN-13 978-981-4261-65-4

Printed by FuIsland Offset Printing (S) Pte Ltd. Singapore

Dedicated with love and respect
to my parents
Shuxiang Wang and Yuhai Liu (God rest his soul),
to Huibo Heidi Ma
to my twin sons
Max Boyang and Louis Boyang,
to whom I owe
all that I am and all that I have accomplished.

Preface

Firewalls are the most critical and widely deployed intrusion prevention systems. A firewall is a security guard placed at the point of entry between a private network and the outside Internet such that all incoming and outgoing packets have to pass through it. The function of a firewall is to examine every incoming or outgoing packet and decide whether to accept or discard it. This function is conventionally specified by a sequence of rules, where rules often conflict. To resolve conflicts, the decision for each packet is the decision of the first rule that the packet matches. Consequently, the rules in a firewall are order sensitive. Because of the conflicts and order sensitivity of firewall rules, firewalls are difficult to design and analyze correctly. It has been observed that most firewalls on the Internet are poorly designed and have many errors in their rules.

Towards the goal of correct firewalls, this book focuses on the following two fundamental problems: first, how to design a new firewall such that the number of errors introduced in the design phase is small; second, how to analyze an existing firewall such that we can detect errors that have been built in. For firewall design, we present two methods for designing stateless firewalls, namely the method of structured firewall design and the method of diverse firewall design, and a model for specifying stateful firewalls. For firewall analysis, we present two methods, namely firewall queries and firewall redundancy detection.

The firewall design and analysis methods presented in this book are not limited to just firewalls. Rather, they are extensible to other rule-based systems such as general packet classification systems and IPsec.

Alex X. Liu

Contents

Chapter 1

Prologue

1.1 Background and Motivation

Firewalls are crucial elements in network security, and have been widely deployed in most businesses and institutions for securing private networks. A firewall is a security guard placed at the point of entry between a private network and the outside Internet such that all incoming and outgoing packets have to pass through it. A packet can be viewed as a tuple with a finite number of fields such as source IP address, destination IP address, source port number, destination port number, and protocol type. By examining the values of these fields for each incoming and outgoing packet, a firewall accepts legitimate packets and discards illegitimate ones according to its configuration. A firewall configuration defines which packets are legitimate and which are illegitimate. An error in a firewall configuration, i.e., a wrong definition of being legitimate or illegitimate for some packets, means that the firewall either accepts some malicious packets, which consequently creates security holes on the firewall, or discards some legitimate packets, which consequently disrupts normal businesses. Given the importance of firewalls, such errors are not acceptable. Unfortunately, it has been observed that most firewalls on the Internet are poorly designed and have many errors in their configurations [Wool (2004)]. Therefore, how to design a new firewall configuration and how to analyze an existing firewall configuration become important issues.

Conventionally, a firewall configuration is specified as a sequence of rules. Each rule in a firewall configuration is of the form

$$\langle predicate \rangle \rightarrow \langle decision \rangle$$

The $\langle predicate \rangle$ of a rule is a boolean expression over some packet fields together with the physical network interface on which a packet arrives. For simplicity, we assume that each packet has a field containing the identifi-cation of the network interface on which a packet arrives. The ⟨*decision*⟩ of a rule can be *accept*, or *discard*, or a combination of these decisions with other options such as a logging option. For simplicity, we assume that the ⟨*decision*⟩ of a rule is either *accept* or *discard*. A packet *matches* a rule if and only if (*iff*) the packet satisfies the predicate of the rule. The rules in a firewall configuration often conflict. Two rules in a firewall configuration *conflict* iff they overlap and also have different decisions. Two rules in a firewall configuration *overlap* iff there is at least one packet that can match both rules. Due to conflicts among rules, a packet may match more than one rule in a firewall configuration, and the rules that a packet matches may have different decisions. To resolve conflicts, the decision for each packet is the decision of the first (i.e., highest priority) rule that the packet matches. Consequently, the rules in a firewall configuration are order sensitive. To ensure that every packet has at least one matching rule in a firewall config-uration, the predicate of the last rule in a firewall configuration is usually a tautology. The last rule of a firewall configuration is usually called the *default rule* of the firewall.

Because of the conflicts and order sensitivity of firewall rules, firewall configurations are difficult to design and analyze correctly. The goal of this book is to reduce firewall configuration errors. We approach this goal from two directions: (1) how to reduce errors when a firewall configuration is being designed, and (2) how to detect errors after a firewall configuration has been designed. In this book, we present two methods for designing firewall configurations, one model for specifying stateful firewalls, and two methods for analyzing firewall configurations.

Since the correctness of a firewall configuration is the focus of this book, we assume a firewall is correct *iff* (if and only if) its configuration is correct, and a firewall configuration is correct iff it satisfies its given requirement specification, which is usually written in a natural language. In the rest of this book, we use "firewall" to mean "firewall configuration" if not otherwise specified.

In this book, for ease of presentation, we assume that a firewall maps every packet to one of two decisions: accept or discard. Most firewall software supports more than two decisions such as accept, accept-and-log, discard, and discard-and-log. Our firewall design and analysis methods can be straightforwardly extended to support more than two decisions.

The firewall design and analysis methods presented in this book are not limited to just firewalls. Rather, they are extensible to other rule-based systems such as general packet classification systems and IPsec. This extension is straightforward.

1.2   Previous Work

Most of previous work on firewalls focuses on improving the performance of firewalls in the area of packet classification [Singh *et al.* (2003); Spitznagel *et al.* (2003); Woo (2000); Qiu *et al.* (2001); Baboescu and Varghese (2001); Baboescu *et al.* (2003); Srinivasan *et al.* (1999, 1998)]. Because the central theme of this book concerns about the correctness of firewalls, below we mainly survey related work in this respect.

1.2.1   *Previous Work on Firewall Design*

Previous work on firewall design focuses on high-level languages that can be used to specify firewall rules. Examples of such languages are the simple model definition language in [Bartal *et al.* (1999, 2003)], the Lisp-like language in [Guttman (1997)], and the declarative predicate language in [Begel *et al.* (1999)]. These high-level firewall languages are helpful for designing firewalls because otherwise people have to use vendor specific languages to describe firewall rules. However, a firewall specified using these high-level firewall languages is still a sequence of rules and the rules may still conflict. The three issues of consistency, completeness and compactness that are inherent in designing a firewall by a sequence of rules still remain.

In comparison, in this book, we present two new firewall design methods: *Structured Firewall Design* and *Diverse Firewall Design*. The Structured Firewall Design method is the first method that addresses all the three issues of consistency, completeness and compactness. The Diverse Firewall Design method is the first method that applies the principle of diverse design to designing firewalls. These two design methods are complementary and prior steps to those high-level firewall languages.

Although a variety of stateful firewall products have been available and deployed on the Internet for some time, such as Cisco PIX Firewalls, Cisco Reflexive ACLs, CheckPoint FireWall-1 and Netfilter/IPTables, no model for specifying stateful firewalls exists. The lack of such a model constitutes a significant impediment for further development of stateful firewall technologies. In this book, we introduce the first model for specifying stateful firewalls. Our model of stateful firewalls has several favorable properties.

First, despite its simplicity, it can express a variety of state tracking functionalities. Second, it allows us to inherit the rich results in stateless firewall design and analysis. Third, it provides backward compatibility such that a stateless firewall can also be specified using our model.

1.2.2 *Previous Work on Firewall Analysis*

Previous work on firewall analysis focuses on conflict detection [Hari *et al.* (2000); Eppstein and Muthukrishnan (2001); Moffett and Sloman (1994); Baboescu and Varghese (2002)], anomaly detection [Al-Shaer and Hamed (2003a,b, 2004)], and firewall queries [Mayer *et al.* (2000); Wool (2001); Hazelhurst *et al.* (2000); Eronen and Zitting (2001)].

The basic idea of firewall conflict detection is to first detect all pairs of rules that conflict, and then the firewall designer manually examines every pair of conflicting rules to see whether the two rules need to be swapped or a new rule needs to be added. Similar to conflict detection, six types of so-called "anomalies" were defined in [Al-Shaer and Hamed (2003a,b, 2004)]. Examining each conflict or anomaly is helpful in reducing errors; however, the number of conflicts in a firewall is usually large, and the manual checking of each conflict or anomaly is unreliable because the meaning of each rule depends on the current order of the rules in the firewall, which may be incorrect.

In [Mayer *et al.* (2000); Wool (2001)], a firewall analysis system that uses some specific firewall queries was presented. However, no algorithm was presented for processing firewall queries. In [Hazelhurst *et al.* (2000)], some ad-hoc "what if" questions that are similar to firewall queries were discussed. Again, no algorithm was presented for processing the proposed "what if" questions. In [Eronen and Zitting (2001)], expert systems were proposed to analyze firewall rules. Clearly, building an expert system just for analyzing a firewall is overwrought and impractical.

There are some tools currently available for network vulnerability testing, such as Satan [Farmer and Venema (1993); Freiss (1998)] and Nessus [Nessus (2004)]. These vulnerability testing tools scan a private network based on the current publicly known attacks, rather than the requirement specification of a firewall. Although these tools can possibly catch errors that allow illegitimate access to the private network, they cannot find the errors that disable legitimate communication between the private network and the outside Internet.

In comparison, in this book, we introduce a simple and effective SQL-like query language, called the Structured Firewall Query Language (SFQL), for describing firewall queries; a theorem, called the Firewall Query Theorem, as a foundation for developing firewall query processing algorithms; and an efficient firewall query processing algorithm.

1.3 Contributions of the Book

Towards the goal of correct firewalls, this book focuses on the following two fundamental problems: how to design a new firewall such that the errors introduced in the design phase is reduced, and how to analyze an existing firewall such that we can detect errors that have been built in. For firewall design, we present two methods for designing stateless firewalls, namely the method of structured firewall design and the method of diverse firewall design, and a model for specifying stateful firewalls. For firewall analysis, we present two methods, namely firewall queries and firewall redundancy detection.

1.3.1 *Structured Firewall Design*

Designing a firewall directly by a sequence of rules suffers from three types of major problems: (1) the consistency problem, which means that it is difficult to order the rules correctly; (2) the completeness problem, which means that it is difficult to ensure thorough consideration for all types of traffic; (3) the compactness problem, which means that it is difficult to keep the number of rules small (because some rules may be redundant and some rules may be combined into one rule).

To achieve consistency, completeness, and compactness, we present a new method called the *Structured Firewall Design* in [Gouda and Liu (2004)], which consists of two steps. First, one designs a firewall using a Firewall Decision Diagram instead of a sequence of often conflicting rules. Second, a program converts the firewall decision diagram into a compact, yet functionally equivalent, sequence of rules.

This method addresses the consistency problem because a firewall decision diagram is conflict-free. It addresses the completeness problem because the syntactic requirements of a firewall decision diagram force the designer to consider all types of traffic. It also addresses the compactness problem because in the second step we first used two algorithms, a standard algorithm for decision diagram reduction and a new algorithm called firewall decision diagram marking, to combine rules together, and then used a new algorithm to remove redundant rules.

1.3.2 *Diverse Firewall Design*

Fundamentally, firewall errors result from human errors. To reduce human errors, we present the method of *Diverse Firewall Design* in [Liu and Gouda (2004)]. This method consists of two phases: a design phase and a comparison phase. In the design phase, the same requirement specification of a firewall is given to multiple teams, who proceed independently to design the firewall. In the comparison phase, the resulting designs from the teams are compared with each other to identify all the discrepancies among them. Each discrepancy is then investigated further and a correction is applied if necessary.

The main technical challenge of this method is how to identify all the discrepancies between two given firewalls. We present a series of three efficient algorithms in this book to solve this problem: (1) a construction algorithm for constructing an equivalent firewall decision tree from a sequence of rules, (2) a shaping algorithm for transforming two firewall decision trees to become semi-isomorphic without changing their semantics, and (3) a comparison algorithm for detecting all the discrepancies between two semi-isomorphic firewall decision trees.

1.3.3 *Stateful Firewall Model*

In order to determine whether a packet should be accepted or discarded, traditional firewalls (i.e., stateless firewalls) examine only the packet itself. In contrast, newer stateful firewalls examine not only the packet but also the state of the firewall. Stateful firewalls can achieve finer access control by tracking the communication state between a private network and the outside Internet. State tracking functionalities in current stateful firewall products, unfortunately, are often hard coded, and different vendors hard code different state tracking functionalities. So far, there is no model for specifying stateful firewalls. Consequently, not only is firewall administrators unable to fully control the function of their firewall, but also it is difficult to design and analyze stateful firewalls.

To facilitate the development of stateful firewalls, in [Gouda and Liu (2005)], we present a simple model for specifying stateful firewalls. Our model of stateful firewalls has several favorable properties. First, despite its simplicity, it can express a variety of state tracking functionalities. Second, it allows us to inherit the rich results in stateless firewall design and analysis. Third, it provides backward compatibility such that a stateless firewall can also be specified using our model. Moreover, we present several methods in [Gouda and Liu (2005)] to analyze the properties of a stateful firewall specified in this model.

1.3.4 *Firewall Queries*

Although a firewall is specified by a mere sequence of rules, understanding its function is by no means an easy task. Even understanding the implication of a single rule is difficult because one has to go through all the rules listed above that rule to figure out their logical relations. Understanding the function of an entire firewall is even more difficult because the firewall may have a large number of rules and the rules often conflict with each other. Furthermore, firewall administrators often have to analyze legacy firewalls that were written by different administrators, at different times, and for different reasons. Effective methods and tools for analyzing firewalls, therefore, are crucial to the success of firewalls.

Firewall queries are questions concerning the function of a firewall. An example firewall query is "Which computers in the private network can receive packets with destination port 1434 and protocol type UDP from the outside Internet?". Such queries are of tremendous help for firewall administrators to understand and analyze the function of their firewalls. For example, the above firewall query example can be used to detect which computers in a private network are vulnerable to Sapphire Worm attacks because Sapphire Worms use UDP port 1434. If the answer to this firewall query is not an empty set, then the firewall administrator may need to modify the firewall to prevent Sapphire Worm attacks.

No algorithm for processing such queries exists in previous literature. In [Liu *et al.* (2004)], we presented a simple and effective SQL-like query language, called the Structured Firewall Query Language (SFQL), for describing firewall queries; a theorem, called the Firewall Query Theorem, as a foundation for developing firewall query processing algorithms; and an efficient firewall query processing algorithm.

1.3.5   *Firewall Redundancy Detection*

Firewalls, especially those that have been updated many times, often contain redundant rules. A rule in a firewall is redundant if and only if removing the rule does not change the function of the firewall. When a firewall consists of many redundant rules, the firewall becomes difficult to manage. A redundant rule may indicate a possible error if the rule is not expected to be redundant. In addition, redundant rules significantly degrade the performance of firewalls, especially TCAM based firewalls. The technical challenge is how to detect all the redundant rules in a firewall. There is no previous solution for this problem. In [Liu and Gouda (2005)], we developed theorems for identifying all the redundant rules in a firewall, and we presented the first algorithm that can detect all the redundant rules in a firewall, which means that in the resulting firewall no rule can be removed without changing the function of the firewall.

1.4   Overview of the Book

The rest of this book proceeds as follows. In Chapter 1.4, we introduce the method of structured firewall design. In Chapter 2.8, we present the method of diverse firewall design. In Chapter 3.4, we show a model for specifying stateful firewalls and some method for analyzing the the properties of stateful firewalls specified in this model. In Chapter 4.5.2, we present how to describe and process firewall queries. In Chapter 5.5, we develop theorems and algorithms for removing all the redundant rules in any given firewall. Finally, in Chapter 6.4, we summarize our research and suggest several topics for future research.

Chapter 2

Structured Firewall Design

The current practice of designing a firewall directly as a sequence of rules suffers from three types of major problems: (1) the consistency problem, which means that it is difficult to order the rules correctly; (2) the completeness problem, which means that it is difficult to ensure thorough consideration for all types of traffic; (3) the compactness problem, which means that it is difficult to keep the number of rules small (because some rules may be redundant and some rules may be combined into one rule).

To achieve consistency, completeness, and compactness, we present a method called *Structured Firewall Design*, which consists of two steps. First, one designs a firewall using a Firewall Decision Diagram instead of a sequence of often conflicting rules. Second, a program converts the firewall decision diagram into a compact, yet functionally equivalent, sequence of rules. This method addresses the consistency problem because a firewall decision diagram is conflict-free. It addresses the completeness problem because the syntactic requirements of a firewall decision diagram force the designer to consider all types of traffic. It also addresses the compactness problem because in the second step we use two algorithms (namely FDD reduction and FDD marking) to combine rules together, and one algorithm (namely Firewall compaction) to remove redundant rules.

2.1 Motivation

2.1.1 *Consistency, Completeness and Compactness*

Because of the conflicts and order sensitivity of firewall rules, designing a firewall directly as a sequence of rules suffers from these three problems: the consistency problem, the completeness problem, and the compactness

9

problem. Next, we expatiate on these three problems via a simple firewall example shown in Figure 2.1. This firewall resides on a gateway router that connects a private network to the outside Internet. The gateway router has two interfaces: interface 0, which connects the router to the outside Internet, and interface 1, which connects the router to the private network. In this example, we assume that every packet has the following five fields.

name	meaning
I	Interface
S	Source IP address
D	Destination IP address
N	Destination Port Number
P	Protocol Type

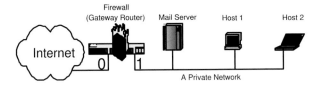

(1) Rule r_1: $(\mathbf{I} = \mathbf{0}) \wedge (\mathbf{S} = \mathbf{any}) \wedge (\mathbf{D} = \mathbf{Mail\ Server}) \wedge (\mathbf{N} = \mathbf{25}) \wedge (\mathbf{P} = \mathbf{tcp}) \rightarrow \mathbf{accept}$
   (This rule allows incoming SMTP packets to proceed to the mail server.)
(2) Rule r_2:
   $(\mathbf{I} = \mathbf{0}) \wedge (\mathbf{S} = \mathbf{Malicious\ Hosts}) \wedge (\mathbf{D} = \mathbf{any}) \wedge (\mathbf{N} = \mathbf{any}) \wedge (\mathbf{P} = \mathbf{any}) \rightarrow \mathbf{discard}$
   (This rule discards incoming packets from previously known malicious hosts.)
(3) Rule r_3: $(\mathbf{I} = \mathbf{1}) \wedge (\mathbf{S} = \mathbf{any}) \wedge (\mathbf{D} = \mathbf{any}) \wedge (\mathbf{N} = \mathbf{any}) \wedge (\mathbf{P} = \mathbf{any}) \rightarrow \mathbf{accept}$
   (This rule allows any outgoing packet to proceed.)
(4) Rule r_4: $(\mathbf{I} = \mathbf{any}) \wedge (\mathbf{S} = \mathbf{any}) \wedge (\mathbf{D} = \mathbf{any}) \wedge (\mathbf{N} = \mathbf{any}) \wedge (\mathbf{P} = \mathbf{any}) \rightarrow \mathbf{accept}$
   (This rule allows any incoming or outgoing packet to proceed.)

Fig. 2.1   A Firewall Example

A firewall on the Internet typically consists of hundreds or thousands of rules. Here for simplicity, this firewall example only has four rules. Although this firewall is small, it exemplifies all the following three problems.

(1) **Consistency Problem**: It is difficult to order the rules in a firewall correctly. This difficulty mainly comes from conflicts among rules. Because rules often conflict, the order of the rules in a firewall is critical. The decision for every packet is the decision of the first rule that the packet matches. In the firewall example in Figure 2.1, rule r_1 and r_2 conflict since the SMTP packets from previously known malicious hosts

to the mail server match both rules and the decisions of r_1 and r_2 are different. Because r_1 is listed before r_2 and the decision of rule r_1 is "*accept*", the SMTP packets from previously known malicious hosts are allowed to proceed to the mail server. However, such packets probably should be prohibited from reaching the mail server because they originate from malicious hosts. Therefore, rules r_1 and r_2 probably should be swapped.

Because of the conflicts, the net effect of a rule cannot be understood by the literal meaning of the rule. The decision of a rule affects the fate of the packets that match this rule but does not match any rule listed before this rule. To understand one single rule r_i, one needs to go through all the rules from r_1 to r_{i-1}, and for every rule r_j, where $1 \le j \le i - 1$, one needs to figure out the logical relationship between the predicate of r_j and that of r_i. In the firewall example in Figure 2.1, the net effect of rule r_2 is not to "discard all packets originated from previously known malicious hosts", but rather is to "discard all non-SMTP packets originated from previously known malicious hosts". The difficulty in understanding firewall rules in turn makes the design and maintenance of a firewall error-prone. Maintenance of a firewall usually involves inserting, deleting or updating rules, and reporting the function of the firewall to others such as managers. All of these tasks require precise understanding of firewalls, which is difficult, especially when the firewall administrator is forced to maintain a legacy firewall that is not originally designed by him.

(2) **Completeness Problem**: It is difficult to ensure that all possible packets are considered. To ensure that every packet has at least one matching rule in a firewall, the common practice is to make the predicate of the last rule a tautology. This is clearly not a good way to ensure the thorough consideration of all possible packets. In the firewall example in Figure 2.1, due to the last rule r_4, non-email packets from the outside to the mail server and email packets from the outside to the hosts other than the mail server are accepted by the firewall. However, these two types of traffic probably should be blocked. A mail server is usually dedicated to email service only. When a host other than the mail server starts to behave like a mail server, it could be an indication that the host has been hacked and it is sending out spam. To block these two types of traffic, the following two rules should be inserted immediately after rule r_1 in the above firewall:

(a) $(I = 0) \wedge (S = any) \wedge (D = Mail\ Server) \wedge (N = any) \wedge (P = any) \rightarrow discard$

(b) $(I = 0) \wedge (S = any) \wedge (D = any) \wedge (N = 25) \wedge (P = tcp) \rightarrow discard$

(3) **Compactness Problem**: A poorly designed firewall often has redundant rules. A rule in a firewall is redundant iff removing the rule does not change the function of the firewall, i.e., does not change the decision of the firewall for every packet. In the above firewall example in Figure 2.1, rule r_3 is redundant. This is because all the packets that match r_3 but do not match r_1 and r_2 also match r_4, and both r_3 and r_4 have the same decision. Therefore, this firewall can be made more compact by removing rule r_3.

The consistency problem and the completeness problem cause firewall errors. An error in a firewall means that the firewall either accepts some malicious packets, which consequently creates security holes on the firewall, or discards some legitimate packets, which consequently disrupts normal businesses. Given the importance of firewalls, such errors are not acceptable. Unfortunately, it has been observed that most firewalls on the Internet are poorly designed and have many errors in their rules [Wool (2004)].

The compactness problem causes low firewall performance. In general, the smaller the number of rules that a firewall has, the faster the firewall can map a packet to the decision of the first rule the packet matches. Reducing the number of rules is especially useful for the firewalls that use TCAM (Ternary Content Addressable Memory). Such firewalls use $O(n)$ space (where n is the number of rules) and constant time in mapping a packet to a decision. Despite the high performance of such TCAM-based firewalls, TCAM has very limited size and consumes much more power as the number of rules increases. Size limitation and power consumption are the two major issues for TCAM-based firewalls.

2.1.2 *Structured Firewall Design*

To achieve consistency, completeness, and compactness, we present a firewall design method called *Structured Firewall Design*, which consists of two steps. First, one designs a firewall using a Firewall Decision Diagram (FDD for short) instead of a sequence of often conflicting rules. Second, a program converts the FDD into a compact, yet functionally equivalent, sequence of rules. This method addresses the consistency problem because an FDD is conflict-free. It addresses the completeness problem because the syntactic requirements of an FDD force the designer to consider all types of traffic. It also addresses the compactness problem because in the second step we use two algorithms (namely FDD reduction and FDD marking) to combine rules together, and one algorithm (namely Firewall compaction) to remove redundant rules.

In some sense, the method of structured firewall design is like the method of structured programming, and the method of designing a firewall directly as a sequence of conflicting rules is like the method of writing a program with many goto statements. In late 1960s, Dijkstra pointed out that goto statements are considered harmful [Dijkstra (1968)] because a program with many goto statements is very difficult to understand and therefore writing such a program is very error prone. Similarly, a firewall of a sequence of conflicting rules is very difficult to understand and writing a sequence of conflicting rules directly is extremely error prone.

Using the method of structured firewall design, the firewall administrator only deals with the FDD that uniquely represents the semantics of a firewall. The FDD is essentially the formal specification of a firewall. Since an FDD can be converted to an equivalent sequence of rules, the method does not require any modification to any existing firewall, which takes a sequence of rules as its configuration. Whenever the firewall administrator wants to change the function of his firewall, he only needs to modify the FDD and then use programs to automatically generate a new sequence of rules. This process is like a programmer first modifying his source code and then compiling it again.

2.2 Firewall Decision Diagrams

A *field* F_i is a variable whose domain, denoted $D(F_i)$, is a finite interval of nonnegative integers. For example, the domain of the source address in an IP packet is $[0, 2^{32} - 1]$.

A *packet* over fields $F_1, \cdots, F_d$ is a d-tuple $(p_1, \cdots, p_d)$ where each p_i $(1 \leq i \leq d)$ is an element of $D(F_i)$. We use Σ to denote the set of all packets over fields $F_1, \cdots, F_d$. It follows that Σ is a finite set and $|\Sigma| = |D(F_1)| \times \cdots \times |D(F_d)|$, where $|\Sigma|$ denotes the number of elements in set Σ and each $|D(F_i)|$ $(1 \leq i \leq d)$ denotes the number of elements in set $D(F_i)$.

Definition 2.2.1 (Firewall Decision Diagram). *A* Firewall Decision

Diagram *(FDD)* f *over fields* $F_1, \cdots, F_d$ *is an acyclic and directed graph that has the following five properties:*

(1) There is exactly one node in f that has no incoming edges. This node is called the root *of f. The nodes in f that have no outgoing edges are called* terminal *nodes of f.*

(2) Each node v in f is labeled with a field, denoted $F(v)$, such that

$$F(v) \in \begin{cases} \{F_1, \cdots, F_d\} & \text{if } v \text{ is nonterminal} \\ \{accept, discard\} & \text{if } v \text{ is terminal.} \end{cases}$$

(3) Each edge e in f is labeled with a nonempty set of integers, denoted $I(e)$, such that if e is an outgoing edge of node v, then we have

$$I(e) \subseteq D(F(v)).$$

(4) A directed path in f from the root to a terminal node is called a decision path. *No two nodes on a decision path have the same label.*

(5) The set of all outgoing edges of a node v in f, denoted $E(v)$, satisfies the following two conditions:

    (a) Consistency: *$I(e) \cap I(e') = \emptyset$ for any two distinct edges e and e' in $E(v)$.*

    (b) Completeness: *$\bigcup_{e \in E(v)} I(e) = D(F(v))$.*   □

Figure 2.2 shows an example of an FDD over two fields F_1 and F_2. The domain of each field is the interval $[1, 10]$. Note that in labelling the terminal nodes, we use letter "a" as a shorthand for "*accept*" and letter "d" as a shorthand for "*discard*". These two notations are carried through the rest of this book.

In this chapter, the label of an edge in an FDD is always represented by the minimum number of non-overlapping integer intervals whose union equals the label of the edge. For example, one outgoing edge of the root is labeled with the set $\{1, 2, 3, 4, 9, 10\}$, which is represented by the two intervals $[1, 4]$ and $[9, 10]$.

For brevity, in the rest of this chapter, we assume that all packets and all FDDs are over the d fields $F_1, \cdots, F_d$ unless otherwise specified.

A firewall decision diagram maps each packet to a decision by testing the packet down the diagram from the root to a terminal node, which indicates the decision of the firewall for the packet. Each nonterminal node in a firewall decision diagram specifies a test of a packet field, and each edge descending from that node corresponds to some possible values of that field.

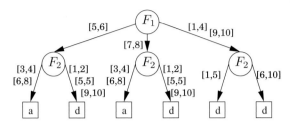

Fig. 2.2   An FDD example

Each packet is mapped to a decision by starting at the root, testing the field that labels this node, then moving down the edge whose label contains the value of the packet field; this process is then repeated for the sub-diagram rooted at the new node.

A decision path in an FDD is represented by $\langle v_1 e_1 \cdots v_k e_k v_{k+1}\rangle$ where v_1 is the root, v_{k+1} is a terminal node, and each e_i $(1 \leq i \leq k)$ is a directed edge from node v_i to node v_{i+1}.

A decision path $\langle v_1 e_1 \cdots v_k e_k v_{k+1}\rangle$ in an FDD represents the following rule:

$$F_1 \in S_1 \wedge \cdots \wedge F_d \in S_d \ \rightarrow \ \langle decision\rangle$$

where

$$S_i = \begin{cases} I(e_j) & \text{if there is a node } v_j \text{ in the decision path that is labeled} \\ & \text{with field } F_i \\ D(F_i) & \text{otherwise} \end{cases}$$

and $\langle decision\rangle$ is the label of the terminal node v_{k+1} in the path.

For an FDD f, we use $f.rules$ to denote the set of all rules that are represented by all the decision paths of f. For any packet p, there is one and only one rule in $f.rules$ that p matches because of the consistency and completeness properties of an FDD. For example, the rules represented by all the decision paths of the FDD in Figure 2.2 are listed in Figure 2.3. Taking the example of the packet $(7, 9)$, it matches only rule r_4 in Figure 2.3.

The semantics of an FDD f is defined as follows: for any packet p, f maps p to the decision of the rule (in fact the only rule) that p matches in $f.rules$. More precisely, a packet $(p_1, \cdots, p_d)$ is *accepted by* an FDD f iff there is a rule of the form

$$F_1 \in S_1 \wedge \cdots \wedge F_d \in S_d \ \rightarrow \ accept$$

r_1: $F_1 \in [5,6] \wedge F_2 \in [3,4] \cup [6,8]$ $\qquad \rightarrow a$
r_2: $F_1 \in [5,6] \wedge F_2 \in [1,2] \cup [5,5] \cup [9,10] \rightarrow d$
r_3: $F_1 \in [7,8] \wedge F_2 \in [3,4] \cup [6,8]$ $\qquad \rightarrow a$
r_4: $F_1 \in [7,8] \wedge F_2 \in [1,2] \cup [5,5] \cup [9,10] \rightarrow d$
r_5: $F_1 \in [1,4] \cup [9,10] \wedge F_2 \in [1,5]$ $\qquad \rightarrow d$
r_6: $F_1 \in [1,4] \cup [9,10] \wedge F_2 \in [6,10]$ $\qquad \rightarrow d$

Fig. 2.3   All rules represented by FDD in Figure 2.2

in $f.rules$ such that the condition $p_1 \in S_1 \wedge \cdots \wedge p_d \in S_d$ holds. Similarly, a packet $(p_1, \cdots, p_d)$ is *discarded by* an FDD f iff there is a rule of the form

$$F_1 \in S_1 \wedge \cdots \wedge F_d \in S_d \rightarrow discard$$

in $f.rules$ such that the condition $p_1 \in S_1 \wedge \cdots \wedge p_d \in S_d$ holds. For example, the packet $(6,8)$ is discarded by the FDD in Figure 2.2 because the rule that this packet matches is rule r_4 in Figure 2.3 and the decision of this rule is "*discard*".

Let f be an FDD. The *accept set* of f, denoted $f.accept$, is the set of all packets that are accepted by f. Similarly, the *discard set* of f, denoted $f.discard$, is the set of all packets that are discarded by f. These two sets associated with an FDD precisely define the semantics of the FDD.

Based on the definitions of accept set and discard set, we have the following theorem. (Recall that Σ denotes the set of all packets over the fields $F_1, \cdots, F_d$.)

Theorem 2.2.1 (Theorem of FDDs). For any FDD f, the following two conditions hold:

(1) $f.accept \cap f.discard = \emptyset$, and
(2) $f.accept \cup f.discard = \Sigma$ □

Two FDDs f and f' are *equivalent* iff they have identical accept sets and identical discard sets, i.e., $f.accept = f'.accept$ and $f.discard = f'.discard$.

There are some similarities between the structure of Firewall Decision Diagrams and that of Interval Decision Diagrams [Strehl and Thiele (2000)], which are mainly used in formal verification. However, there are two major differences. First, in a firewall decision diagram, the label of a nonterminal node must have a finite domain; while in an interval decision diagram, the label of a nonterminal node may have an infinite domain. Second, in a firewall decision diagram, the label of an edge is a set of integers which could be the union of several noncontinuous intervals; while in an interval decision diagram, the label of an edge is limited to only one interval. In broader sense, the structure of Firewall Decision Diagrams is also similar to other types of decision diagrams such as the Binary Decision Diagrams [Bryant (1986)] and Decision Trees [Quinlan (1986)]. But note that the optimization goal of reducing the total number of simple rules generated is unique to firewall decision diagrams, which will be explored next.

2.3 FDD Reduction

In this section, we present an algorithm for reducing the number of decision paths in an FDD. This reduction helps to reduce the number of rules generated from an FDD. First, we introduce two concepts: isomorphic nodes in an FDD and reduced FDDs.

Two nodes v and v' in an FDD are *isomorphic* iff v and v' satisfy one of the following two conditions:

(1) Both v and v' are terminal nodes with identical labels.
(2) Both v and v' are nonterminal nodes and there is a one-to-one correspondence between the outgoing edges of v and the outgoing edges of v' such that every pair of corresponding edges have identical labels and they both point to the same node.

An FDD f is *reduced* iff it satisfies all of the following three conditions:

(1) No node in f has only one outgoing edge.
(2) No two nodes in f are isomorphic.
(3) No two nodes have more than one edge between them.

Algorithm 1 (FDD reduction) in Figure 2.4 takes any FDD and outputs an equivalent but reduced FDD. The correctness of this algorithm follows directly from the semantics of FDDs. Note that this algorithm for reducing an FDD is similar to the one described in [Bryant (1986)] for reducing a BDD.

As an example, if we apply Algorithm 1 to the FDD in Figure 2.2, we get the reduced FDD in Figure 2.5. Note that the FDD in Figure 2.2 consists of six decision paths, whereas the FDD in Figure 2.5 consists of three decision paths.

Algorithm 1 (FDD Reduction)
Input   : An FDD f
Output : A reduced FDD that is equivalent to f
Steps:

Repeatedly apply the following three reductions to f until none of them can be applied any further.

(1) If there is a node v that has only one outgoing edge e, assuming e points to node v', then remove both node v and edge e, and let all the edges that point to v point to v'.

(2) If there are two nodes v and v' that are isomorphic, then remove v' together with all its outgoing edges, and let all the edges that point to v' point to v.

(3) If there are two edges e and e' that both are between a pair of two nodes, then remove e' and change the label of e from $I(e)$ to $I(e) \cup I(e')$. (Recall that $I(e)$ denotes the label of edge e.)

Fig. 2.4   Algorithm 1 (FDD Reduction)

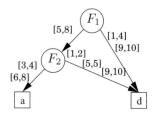

Fig. 2.5   A reduced FDD

2.4   FDD Marking

A firewall rule of the form $F_1 \in S_1 \land \cdots \land F_d \in S_d \rightarrow \langle decision \rangle$ is *simple* iff every S_i ($1 \le i \le d$) is a nonnegative integer interval. Because most firewalls require simple rules, we want to minimize the number of simple rules generated from an FDD. The number of simple rules generated from a "marked version" of an FDD is less than or equal to the number of simple rules generated from the original FDD. Next, we define a marked FDD.

A *marked version* f' of an FDD f is the same as f except that exactly one outgoing edge of each nonterminal node in f' is marked "*all*". Since the labels of the edges that are marked "*all*" do not change, the two FDDs f and f' have the same semantics, i.e., f and f' are equivalent. A marked version of an FDD is also called a *marked FDD*.

Figure 2.6 shows two marked versions f' and f'' of the FDD in Figure 2.5. In f', the edge labeled $[5, 8]$ and the edge labeled $[1, 2] \cup [5, 5] \cup [9, 10]$ are both marked *all*. In f'', the edge labeled $[1, 4] \cup [9, 10]$ and the edge labeled $[1, 2] \cup [5, 5] \cup [9, 10]$ are both marked *all*.

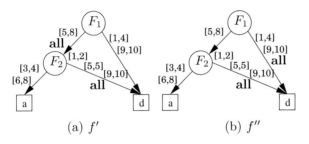

(a) f' (b) f''

Fig. 2.6   Two marked FDDs

The *load of a nonempty set of integers* S, denoted $load(S)$, is the minimal number of non-overlapping integer intervals that cover S. For example, the load of the set $\{1, 2, 3, 5, 8, 9, 10\}$ is 3 because this set is covered by the three integer intervals $[1, 3]$, $[5, 5]$ and $[8, 10]$, and this set cannot be covered by any two intervals.

The *load of an edge* e in a marked FDD, denoted $load(e)$, is defined as follows:

$$load(e) = \begin{cases} 1 & \text{if } e \text{ is marked } all \\ load(I(e)) & \text{otherwise} \end{cases}$$

The *load of a node* v in a marked FDD, denoted $load(v)$, is defined recursively as follows:

$$load(v) = \begin{cases} 1 & \text{if } v \text{ is terminal} \\ \sum_{i=1}^{k}(load(e_i) \times load(v_i)) & \text{if } v \text{ is nonterminal: suppose } v \text{ has } k \\ & \text{outgoing edges } e_1, \cdots, e_k, \text{ which} \\ & \text{point to nodes } v_1, \cdots, v_k \\ & \text{respectively} \end{cases}$$

The *load of a marked FDD* f, denoted $load(f)$, equals the load of the root of f.

Different marked versions of the same FDD may have different loads. Figure 2.6 shows two marked versions f' and f'' of the same FDD in Figure 2.5. The load of f' is 5, whereas the load of f'' is 4.

As we will see in Section 2.7, for any two marked versions of the same FDD, the one with the smaller load will generate a smaller number of simple rules. Therefore, we should use the marked version of FDD f that has the minimal load to generate rules.

Algorithm 2 (FDD marking) in Figure 2.7 takes any FDD and outputs a marked version that has the minimal load.

Algorithm 2 (FDD Marking)
Input   : An FDD f
Output : A marked version f' of f such that for every marked version f''
            of f, $load(f') \leq load(f'')$
Steps:

(1) Compute the load of each terminal node v in f as follows: $load(v) := 1$
(2) **while** there is a node v whose load has not yet been computed, suppose v has k outgoing edges $e_1, \cdots, e_k$ and these edges point to nodes $v_1, \cdots, v_k$ respectively, and the loads of these k nodes have been computed
    do

   (a) Among the k edges $e_1, \cdots, e_k$, choose an edge e_j with the largest value of $(load(e_j) - 1) \times load(v_j)$, and mark edge e_j with "*all*".
   (b) Compute the load of v as follows: $load(v) := \sum_{i=1}^{k}(load(e_i) \times load(v_i))$.

    end

Fig. 2.7   Algorithm 2 (FDD Marking)

As an example, if we apply Algorithm 2 to the reduced FDD in Figure 2.5, we get the marked FDD in Figure 2.6(b).

The correctness of Algorithm 2 is stated in Theorem 2.4.1.

Theorem 2.4.1. The load of an FDD marked by Algorithm 2 (FDD Marking) is minimal.   □

Proof of Theorem 2.4.1 Consider an FDD f. Let f' be the version marked by algorithm 2, and let f'' be an arbitrary marked version. Next we prove that $load(f') \leq load(f'')$.

Consider a node v, which has k outgoing edges $e_1, e_2, \cdots, e_k$ and these edges point to $v_1, v_2, \cdots, v_k$ respectively, such that the loads of $v_1, v_2, \cdots, v_k$ in f' is the same as those in f''. Clearly such node v exists because the load of any terminal node is constant 1.

Let e_i be the edge marked *ALL* in f' and e_j be the edge marked *ALL* in f''. Suppose $i \neq j$. We use $load'(v)$ to denote the load of node v in f' and $load''(v)$ to denote the load of node v in f''. We then have

$$load'(v) = \sum_{t=1}^{i-1}(load(e_t) \times load(v_t)) + load(v_i) + \sum_{t=i+1}^{k}(load(e_t) \times load(v_t))$$
$$load''(v) = \sum_{t=1}^{j-1}(load(e_t) \times load(v_t)) + load(v_j) + \sum_{t=j+1}^{k}(load(e_t) \times load(v_t))$$
$$load'(v) - load''(v) = (load(e_j) - 1) \times load(v_j) - (load(e_i) - 1) \times load(v_i)$$

According to Algorithm 2, $(load(e_j) - 1) \times load(v_j) \leq (load(e_i) - 1) \times load(v_i)$. So, $load'(v) \leq load''(v)$.

Apply the above argument to any node v in f, we have $load'(v) \leq load''(v)$. So, the load of an FDD marked by Algorithm 2 is minimal. $\quad\square$

2.5 Firewall Generation

In this section, we present an algorithm for generating a sequence of rules, which form a firewall, from a marked FDD such that the firewall has the same semantics as the marked FDD. First, we introduce the semantics of a firewall.

A packet $(p_1, \cdots, p_d)$ matches a rule $F_1 \in S_1 \wedge \cdots \wedge F_d \in S_d \rightarrow \langle decision \rangle$ iff the condition $p_1 \in S_1 \wedge \cdots \wedge p_d \in S_d$ holds. A *firewall* consists of a sequence of rules such that for any packet there is at least one rule that the packet matches. A firewall maps every packet to the decision of the first rule that the packet matches. Let f be a firewall of a sequence of rules. The set of all packets accepted by f is denoted $f.accept$, and the set of all packets discarded by f is denoted $f.discard$. The next theorem follows from these definitions. Recall that Σ denotes the set of all packets over the fields $F_1, \cdots, F_d$.

Theorem 2.5.1 (Theorem of Firewalls). For a firewall f of a sequence of rules,

(1) $f.accept \cap f.discard = \emptyset$, and
(2) $f.accept \cup f.discard = \Sigma$ $\quad\square$

Based on Theorem 2.2.1 and 2.5.1, we now extend the equivalence relations on FDDs to incorporate the firewalls. Given f and f', where each is an FDD or a firewall, f and f' are *equivalent* iff they have identical accept sets and identical discard sets, i.e., $f.accept = f'.accept$ and $f.discard = f'.discard$. This equivalence relation is symmetric, reflexive, and transitive. We use $f \equiv f'$ to denote the equivalence relation between f and f'.

To generate an equivalent firewall from a marked FDD f, we basically make a depth-first traversal of f such that for each nonterminal node v, the outgoing edge marked "*all*" of v is traversed after all the other outgoing edges of v have been traversed. Whenever a terminal node is encountered, assuming $\langle v_1 e_1 \cdots v_k e_k v_{k+1} \rangle$ is the decision path where for every i ($1 \leq i \leq k$) e_i is the most recently traversed outgoing edge of node v_i, output a rule r as follows:

$$F_1 \in S_1 \wedge \cdots \wedge F_d \in S_d \;\rightarrow\; F(v_{k+1})$$

where

$$S_i = \begin{cases} I(e_j) & \text{if the decision path has a node } v_j \text{ that is labeled with field } F_i \\ & \text{and } e_j \text{ *is not marked* "all"} \\ \\ D(F_i) & \text{otherwise} \end{cases}$$

Note that the i-th rule output is the i-th rule in the firewall generated.

For the above rule r, the predicate $F_1 \in S_1 \wedge \cdots \wedge F_d \in S_d$ is called the *matching predicate* of r.

The rule represented by the path $\langle v_1 e_1 \cdots v_k e_k v_{k+1} \rangle$ is $F_1 \in T_1 \wedge \cdots \wedge F_d \in T_d \;\rightarrow\; F(v_{k+1})$, where

$$T_i = \begin{cases} I(e_j) & \text{if the decision path has a node } v_j \text{ that is labeled with field } F_i \\ \\ D(F_i) & \text{otherwise} \end{cases}$$

We call the predicate $F_1 \in T_1 \wedge \cdots \wedge F_d \in T_d$ the *resolving predicate* of the above rule r. Note that if a packet satisfies the resolving predicate of r, r is the first rule that the packet matches in the firewall generated. If a packet satisfies the resolving predicate of rule r in firewall f, we say the packet is *resolved* by r in f.

Algorithm 3 (firewall generation) in Figure 2.8 takes any marked FDD and outputs an equivalent firewall. Recall that the i-th rule output by Algorithm 3 is the i-th rule in the firewall generated. The correctness of this algorithm follows directly from the semantics of FDDs and firewalls. In

Algorithm 3, for every rule generated, we also generate its matching predicate and its resolving predicate. In the next section, we will see that these two predicates associated with each rule play important roles in removing redundant rules.

Algorithm 3 (Firewall Generation)
Input   : A marked FDD f
Output : A firewall that is equivalent to f. For each rule r, $r.mp$ and $r.rp$
             is computed
Steps:

Depth-first traverse f such that for each nonterminal node v, the outgoing edge marked "*all*" of v is traversed after all other outgoing edges of v have been traversed. Whenever a terminal node is encountered, assuming $\langle v_1 e_1 \cdots v_k e_k v_{k+1} \rangle$ is the decision path where each e_i is the most recently traversed outgoing edge of node v_i, output a rule r together with its matching predicate $r.mp$ and its resolving predicate $r.rp$ as follows:

r is the rule $F_1 \in S_1 \wedge \cdots \wedge F_d \in S_d \rightarrow F(v_{k+1})$, where

$$S_i = \begin{cases} I(e_j) & \text{if the decision path has a node } v_j \text{ that is labeled with field } F_i \\ & \text{and } e_j \text{ is not marked "all"} \\ D(F_i) & \text{otherwise} \end{cases}$$

$r.mp$ is the predicate of rule r.
$r.rp$ is the predicate $F_1 \in T_1 \wedge \cdots \wedge F_d \in T_d$, where

$$T_i = \begin{cases} I(e_j) & \text{if the decision path has a node } v_j \text{ that is labeled with field } F_i \\ D(F_i) & \text{otherwise} \end{cases}$$

Fig. 2.8   Algorithm 3 (Firewall Generation)

As an example, if we apply Algorithm 3 to the marked FDD in Figure 2.6(b), we get the firewall in Figure 2.9.

2.6   Firewall Compaction

Firewalls often have redundant rules. A rule in a firewall is redundant iff removing the rule does not change the semantics of the firewall, i.e., does not change the accept set and the discard set of the firewall. Removing

$$r_1 \quad = F_1 \in [5,8] \land F_2 \in [3,4] \cup [6,8] \to a,$$
$$r_1.mp = F_1 \in [5,8] \land F_2 \in [3,4] \cup [6,8]$$
$$r_1.rp = F_1 \in [5,8] \land F_2 \in [3,4] \cup [6,8]$$

$$r_2 \quad = F_1 \in [5,8] \land F_2 \in [1,10] \qquad \to d,$$
$$r_2.mp = F_1 \in [5,8] \land F_2 \in [1,10]$$
$$r_2.rp = (F_1 \in [5,8] \land F_2 \in [1,2] \cup [5,5] \cup [9,10])$$

$$r_3 \quad = F_1 \in [1,10] \land F_2 \in [1,10] \qquad \to d,$$
$$r_3.mp = F_1 \in [1,10] \land F_2 \in [1,10]$$
$$r_3.rp = F_1 \in [1,4] \cup [9,10] \land F_2 \in [1,10]$$

Fig. 2.9   A generated firewall

redundant rules from a firewall produces an equivalent firewall but with fewer rules. For example, the rule r_2 in Figure 2.9 is redundant. Removing this rule yields an equivalent firewall with two rules, which are shown in Figure 2.10.

(1) $F_1 \in [5,8] \land F_2 \in [3,4] \cup [6,8] \to a,$
(2) $F_1 \in [1,10] \land F_2 \in [1,10] \to d$

Fig. 2.10   A firewall with no redundant rules

In this section, we present an efficient algorithm for discovering redundant rules. Algorithm 4 (firewall compaction) in Figure 2.11 takes any firewall and outputs an equivalent but more compact firewall.

In Algorithm 4, "$r_i.rp$ implies $r_k.mp$" means that for any packet p, if p satisfies $r_i.rp$, then p satisfies $r_k.mp$. Checking whether $r_i.rp$ implies $r_k.mp$ is simple. Let $r_i.rp$ be $F_1 \in T_1 \land F_2 \in T_2 \land \cdots \land F_d \in T_d$ and let $r_k.mp$ be $F_1 \in S_1 \land F_2 \in S_2 \land \cdots \land F_d \in S_d$. Then, $r_i.rp$ implies $r_k.mp$ iff for every j, where $1 \le j \le d$, the condition $T_j \subseteq S_j$ holds.

Checking whether no packet satisfies both $r_i.rp$ and $r_j.mp$ is simple. Let $r_i.rp$ be $F_1 \in T_1 \land F_2 \in T_2 \land \cdots \land F_d \in T_d$ and let $r_j.mp$ be $F_1 \in S_1 \land F_2 \in S_2 \land \cdots \land F_d \in S_d$. We have $r_i.rp \land r_j.mp = F_1 \in (T_1 \cap S_1) \land F_2 \in (T_2 \cap S_2) \land \cdots \land F_d \in (T_d \cap S_d)$. Therefore, no packet satisfies both $r_i.rp$ and $r_j.mp$ iff there exists j, where $1 \le j \le d$, such that $T_j \cap S_j = \emptyset$.

As an example, if we apply Algorithm 4 to the firewall in Figure 2.9, we get the compact firewall in Figure 2.10.

Algorithm 4 (Firewall Compaction)
Input   : A firewall $\langle r_1, \cdots, r_n \rangle$
Output : An equivalent but more compact firewall
Steps:
1. **for** $i = n$ **to** 1 **do**
    $redundant[i] :=$ **false**.
2. **for** $i = n$ **to** 1 **do**
    if there exist a rule r_k in the firewall, where $i < k \leq n$, such that the
    following four conditions hold
       (1) $redundant[k] = false$.
       (2) r_i and r_k have the same decision.
       (3) $r_i.rp$ implies $r_k.mp$.
       (4) for every rule r_j, where $i < j < k$, at least one of the following
          three conditions holds:
           (a) $redundant[j] = true$.
           (b) r_i and r_j have the same decision.
           (c) no packet satisfies both $r_i.rp$ and $r_j.mp$.
    then $redundant[i] :=$ **true**.
    else $redundant[i] :=$ **false**.
3. **for** $i = n$ **to** 1 **do**
    if $redundant[i] = true$ **then** remove r_i from the firewall.

Fig. 2.11   Algorithm 4 (Firewall Compaction)

Let n be the number of rules in a firewall and d be the number of
packet fields that a rule checks, the computational complexity of Algorithm
4 is $O(n^2 * d)$. Note that d can be regarded as a constant because d is
usually small. Most firewalls checks five packet fields: source IP address,
destination IP address, source port number, destination port number, and
protocol type.
   The correctness of Algorithm 4 is stated in Theorem 2.6.1.

Theorem 2.6.1. If we apply Algorithm 4 to a firewall f and get the resulting firewall f', then f and f' are equivalent.   □

Proof of Theorem 2.6.1: Suppose for the rule r_i in firewall $\langle r_1, \cdots, r_n \rangle$,
there exist a rule r_k in this firewall, where $i < k \leq n$, such that the following
four conditions hold:

(1) $redundant[k] = false$.

(2) r_i and r_k have the same decision.

(3) $r_i.rp$ implies $r_k.mp$.

(4) for every rule r_j, where $i < j < k$, at least one of the following three conditions holds:

    (a) $redundant[j] = true$.

    (b) r_i and r_j have the same decision.

    (c) no packet satisfies both $r_i.rp$ and $r_j.mp$.

If we remove rule r_i from firewall $\langle r_1, \cdots, r_n \rangle$, the packets whose decision may be affected are the packets that are resolved by r_i in $\langle r_1, \cdots, r_n \rangle$, i.e., the packets that satisfy $r_i.rp$. Let S be the set of all the packets that satisfy $r_i.rp$. Because $r_i.rp$ implies $r_k.mp$ and $redundant[k] = false$, if we remove rule r_i, the packets in S will be resolved by the rules from r_{i+1} to r_k in $\langle r_1, \cdots, r_{i-1}, r_{i+1}, \cdots, r_n \rangle$. Consider a rule r_j where $i < j < k$. If $redundant[j] = true$, we assume r_j has been removed; therefore, rule r_j does not affect the decision of any packet in S. If the two rules r_i and r_j have the same decision, then rule r_j does not affect the decision of any packet in S. If no packet satisfies both $r_i.rp$ and $r_j.mp$, then any packet in S does not match rule r_j; therefore, rule r_j does not affect the decision of any packet in S. Note that r_i and r_k have the same decision. Therefore, for any packet p in S, the decision that the firewall $\langle r_1, \cdots, r_{i-1}, r_{i+1}, \cdots, r_n \rangle$ makes for p is the same as the decision that the firewall $\langle r_1, \cdots, r_{i-1}, r_i, r_{i+1}, \cdots, r_n \rangle$ makes for p. So rule r_i is redundant.

Suppose we apply Algorithm 4 to a firewall f. Since any rule removed by Algorithm 4 is redundant, the resulting firewall f' is equivalent to the original firewall f. $\qquad\square$

2.7 Firewall Simplification

Most firewall software, such as Linux's ipchains, requires each firewall rule to be simple. A firewall rule of the form $F_1 \in S_1 \land \cdots \land F_d \in S_d \rightarrow \langle decision \rangle$ is *simple* iff every S_i ($1 \le i \le d$) is an interval of consecutive nonnegative integers. A firewall is *simple* iff all its rules are simple.

Algorithm 5 (firewall simplification) in Figure 2.12 takes any firewall and outputs an equivalent firewall in which each rule is simple. The correctness of this algorithm follows directly from the semantics of firewalls.

As an example, if we apply Algorithm 5 to the firewall in Figure 2.10,

Algorithm 5 (Firewall Simplification)
Input   : A firewall f
Output : A simple firewall f' where f' is equivalent to f
Steps:

while f has a rule of the form $F_1 \in S_1 \wedge \cdots \wedge F_i \in S_i \wedge \cdots \wedge F_d \in S_d \rightarrow \langle decision \rangle$ where some S_i is represented by $[a_1, b_1] \cup \cdots \cup [a_k, b_k]$ where $k \geq 2$.

do

    replace this rule by the following k non-overlapping rules:

$$F_1 \in S_1 \wedge \cdots \wedge F_i \in [a_1, b_1] \wedge \cdots \wedge F_d \in S_d \rightarrow \langle decision \rangle,$$
$$F_1 \in S_1 \wedge \cdots \wedge F_i \in [a_2, b_2] \wedge \cdots \wedge F_d \in S_d \rightarrow \langle decision \rangle,$$
$$\vdots$$
$$F_1 \in S_1 \wedge \cdots \wedge F_i \in [a_k, b_k] \wedge \cdots \wedge F_d \in S_d \rightarrow \langle decision \rangle$$

end

Fig. 2.12   Algorithm 5 (Firewall Simplification)

we get the firewall in Figure 2.13.

(1) $F_1 \in [5, 8] \wedge F_2 \in [3, 4] \rightarrow a,$
(2) $F_1 \in [5, 8] \wedge F_2 \in [6, 8] \rightarrow a,$
(3) $F_1 \in [1, 10] \wedge F_2 \in [1, 10] \rightarrow d,$

Fig. 2.13   A simple firewall

What we get from Algorithm 5 is a simple firewall. For each rule $F_1 \in S_1 \wedge \cdots \wedge F_i \in S_i \wedge \cdots \wedge F_d \in S_d \rightarrow \langle decision \rangle$, S_i is an interval of nonnegative integers. Some existing firewall products, such as Linux's ipchains, require that S_i be represented in a prefix format such as 192.168.0.0/16, where 16 means that the prefix is the first 16 bits of 192.168.0.0 in a binary format. In this chapter we stop the level of discussion at simple rules because an integer interval can be converted to multiple prefixes algorithmically. For example, integer interval $[2, 8]$ can be converted to 3 prefixes: $001*, 01*, 1000$. A $w-$bit integer interval can be converted to at most $2w - 2$ prefixes [Gupta and McKeown (2001)].

2.8   Summary of Structured Firewall Design

In this section, we summarize the firewall design method. Figure 2.14 shows the five steps of this method.

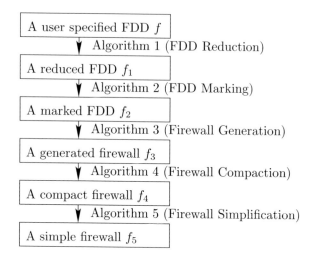

Fig. 2.14   Five steps of the firewall design method ($f \equiv f_1 \equiv f_2 \equiv f_3 \equiv f_4 \equiv f_5$)

The firewall design method starts by a user specifying an FDD f. The consistency and completeness properties of f can be verified automatically based on the syntactic requirements of an FDD. After an FDD is specified, it goes through the following five steps, and we get a simple firewall that is equivalent to the FDD. The first step is to apply Algorithm 1 (FDD Reduction) to the user specified FDD. We then get an equivalent but reduced FDD, which has a smaller number of decision paths. The second step is to apply Algorithm 2 (FDD Marking) to the reduced FDD. We then get an equivalent FDD where each nonterminal node has exactly one outgoing edge that is marked *all*. The third step is to apply Algorithm 3 (FDD Generation) to the marked FDD. We then get an equivalent firewall. The fourth step is to apply Algorithm 4 (Firewall Compaction) to the generated firewall. We then get an equivalent firewall with a smaller number of rules. The fifth step is to apply Algorithm 5 (Firewall Simplification) to this firewall. We then get the final result: a simple firewall that is equivalent to the user specified FDD.

Three of the above five algorithms, namely Algorithm 1 (FDD Reduction), Algorithm 2 (FDD Marking) and Algorithm 4 (Firewall Compaction), are for the purpose of reducing the number of rules in the final simple firewall. Algorithm 1 (FDD Reduction) does so by reducing the number of decision paths in the user specified FDD. Algorithm 2 (FDD Marking) does so by reducing the load of some edges in the FDD. Algorithm 4 (Firewall Compaction) does so by removing some redundant rules from the generated firewall. These three algorithms could reduce the number of simple rules dramatically. Consider the running example illustrated in Figures 2.2 through 2.13. If we directly generate and simplify the firewall from the FDD in Figure 2.2, ignoring Algorithm 1, 2, and 4, we would have ended up with a simple firewall that has 14 rules. However, with the help of these three algorithms, we end up with a simple firewall that has only 3 rules.

Chapter 3

Diverse Firewall Design

We categorize firewall errors into specification induced errors and design induced errors. Specification induced errors are caused by the inherent ambiguities of informal requirement specifications, especially if the requirement specification is written in a natural language. Design induced errors are caused by the technical incapacity of individual firewall designers. We observe that different designers may have different understandings of the same informal requirement specification, and different designers may exhibit different technical strengths and weaknesses. This observation motivates the method of diverse firewall design.

The diverse firewall design method has two phases: a design phase and a comparison phase. In the design phase, the same requirement specification is given to multiple teams who proceed independently to design different versions of the firewall. Different teams preferably have different technical strengths and use different design methods. By maximizing diversity in the design phase, the coincident errors made by all teams are rare. In the comparison phase, the resulting multiple versions are compared with each other to discover all discrepancies. Then each discrepancy is further investigated and a correction is applied if necessary. After these comparisons and corrections, all the versions become equivalent. Then any one of them can be deployed.

The technical challenge in this diverse firewall design method is that how to discover all the functional discrepancies between two given firewalls, where each is designed by either a sequence of rules or a firewall decision diagram. The solution for comparing two given firewalls consists of the following three steps: (1) If either of the two firewalls is designed as a sequence of rules, we construct an equivalent ordered firewall decision diagram from the sequence of rules using the construction algorithm in Section 3.1. If either of the two firewalls is designed as a non-ordered firewall decision diagram, we at first generate an equivalent sequence of rules from the diagram, then construct an equivalent ordered firewall decision diagram from the sequence of rules. After this step, we get two ordered firewall decision diagrams. (2) We transform the two firewall decision diagrams to two semi-isomorphic firewall decision diagrams without changing their semantics using the shaping algorithm in Section 3.2. After this step, we get two semi-isomorphic firewall decision diagrams. (3) We discover all the discrepancies between the two semi-isomorphic firewall decision diagrams using the comparison algorithm in Section 3.3.

The experimental results in Section 3.4 shows that these three algorithms, namely the FDD construction algorithm, the FDD shaping algorithm, and the FDD comparison algorithm, are very efficient. Note that it is fairly straightforward to extend the algorithms for comparing two firewalls to compare N firewalls where $N > 2$.

The idea of diverse firewall design is inspired by N-version programming [Avizienis (1985, 1995); Avizienis and Chen (1977); Teng and Pham (2002)], and back-to-back testing [Vouk (1988a,b)]. The basic idea of N-version programming is to give the same requirement specification to N teams to independently design and implement N programs using different algorithms, languages, or tools. Then the resulting N programs are executed in parallel. A decision mechanism is deployed to examine the N results for each input from the N programs and selects a correct or "best" result. The key element of N-version programming is design diversity. The diversity in the N programs should be maximized such that coincident failure for the same input is rare. The effectiveness of N-version programming method for building fault-tolerant software has been shown in a variety of safety-critical systems built since the 1970s, such as railway interlocking and train control [Anderson and Hagelin (1981)], Airbus flight control [Traverse (1988)], and nuclear reactor protection [Condor and Hinton (1988)].

Back-to-back testing is a complementary method to N-version programming. This method is used to test the resulting N versions before deploying them in parallel. The basic idea is as follows. At first, create a suite of test cases. Second, for each test case, execute the N programs in parallel; cross-compare the N results; then investigate each discrepancy discovered, and apply corrections if necessary.

The diverse firewall design method has two unique properties that distinguish it from N-version programming and back-to-back testing. First, only one firewall version needs to be deployed and executed. This is because all the discrepancies between the multiple firewall versions can be discovered by the algorithms presented in this chapter, and corrections can be applied to make them equivalent. By contrast, the N-version programming method requires the deployment of all the N programs and executing them in parallel. Second, the algorithms in this chapter can detect all the discrepancies between the multiple firewall versions. By contrast, back-to-back testing is not guaranteed to detect all the discrepancies among N programs.

In this chapter, we use the following running example. Consider the simple network in Figure 3.1. This network has a gateway router with two interfaces: interface 0, which connects the gateway router to the outside Internet, and interface 1, which connects the gateway router to the inside local network. The firewall for this local network resides in the gateway router. The requirement specification for this firewall is depicted in Figure 3.2.

Suppose we give this specification to two teams: Team A and Team B. Team A designs the firewall by the FDD in Figure 3.3 and Team B designs the firewall by the sequence of rules in Figure 3.4. In this chapter, we use the following shorthand: a (Accept), d (Discard), I (Interface), S (Source IP), D (Destination IP), N (Destination Port), P (Protocol Type). We use α to denote the integer formed by the four bytes of the IP address 192.168.0.0, and similarly β for 192.168.255.255, and γ for 192.1.2.3. We assume the protocol type value in a packet is either 0 (TCP) or 1 (UDP). For ease of presentation, we assume that each packet has a field containing the information of the network interface on which a packet arrives.

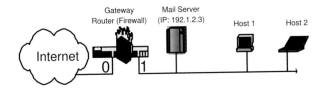

Fig. 3.1 A firewall

Given these two firewalls, one in Figure 3.3 and the other in in Figure 3.4, we use the following three steps to discover all the discrepancies between them: (1) construct an equivalent ordered FDD (in Figure 3.6) from the sequence of rules in Figure 3.4 using the construction algorithm in Section

The mail server with IP address 192.1.2.3 can receive emails. The packets from an outside malicious domain 192.168.0.0/16 should be blocked. Other packets should be accepted and allowed to proceed.

Fig. 3.2   The requirement specification

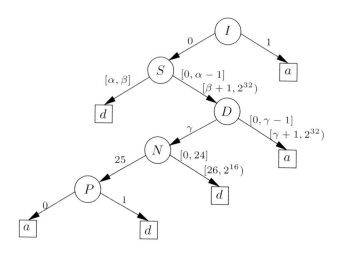

Fig. 3.3   The FDD by Team A

(1) $(I \in \{0\}) \wedge (S \in all) \wedge (D \in \{\gamma\}) \wedge (N \in \{25\}) \wedge (P \in \{0\}) \rightarrow a$
(2) $(I \in \{0\}) \wedge (S \in [\alpha, \beta]) \wedge (D \in all) \wedge (N \in all) \wedge (P \in all) \rightarrow d$
(3) $(I \in all) \wedge (S \in all) \wedge (D \in all) \wedge (N \in all) \wedge (P \in all) \rightarrow a$

Fig. 3.4   The Firewall by Team B

3.1; (2) transform the two ordered FDDs, one in Figure 3.3 and the other in Figure 3.6, to two semi-isomorphic FDDs (where one is in Figure 3.9) using the shaping algorithm in Section 3.2; (3) discover all the discrepancies between the two semi-isomorphic FDDs using the comparison algorithm in Section 3.3.

3.1 Construction Algorithm

In this section, we discuss how to construct an equivalent FDD from a sequence of rules $\langle r_1, \cdots, r_n \rangle$, where each rule is of the format $(F_1 \in S_1) \wedge \cdots \wedge (F_d \in S_d) \rightarrow \langle decision \rangle$. Note that all the d packet fields appear in the predicate of each rule, and they appear in the same order.

We first construct a partial FDD from the first rule. A *partial FDD* is a diagram that has all the properties of an FDD except the completeness property. The partial FDD constructed from a single rule contains only the decision path that defines the rule. Suppose from the first i rules, r_1 through r_i, we have constructed a partial FDD, whose root v is labelled F_1, and suppose v has k outgoing edges $e_1, \cdots, e_k$. Let r_{i+1} be the rule $(F_1 \in S_1) \wedge \cdots \wedge (F_d \in S_d) \rightarrow \langle decision \rangle$. Next we consider how to append rule r_{i+1} to this partial FDD.

At first, we examine whether we need to add another outgoing edge to v. If $S_1 - (I(e_1) \cup \cdots \cup I(e_k)) \neq \emptyset$, we need to add a new outgoing edge with label $S_1 - (I(e_1) \cup \cdots \cup I(e_k))$ to v because any packet whose F_1 field is an element of $S_1 - (I(e_1) \cdots \cup I(e_k))$ does not match any of the first i rules, but matches r_{i+1} provided that the packet satisfies $(F_2 \in S_2) \wedge \cdots \wedge (F_d \in S_d)$. Then we build a decision path from $(F_2 \in S_2) \wedge \cdots \wedge (F_d \in S_d) \rightarrow \langle decision \rangle$, and make the new edge of the node v point to the first node of this decision path.

Second, we compare S_1 and $I(e_j)$ for each j where $1 \leq j \leq k$. This comparison leads to one of the following three cases:

(1) $S_1 \cap I(e_j) = \emptyset$: In this case, we skip edge e_j because any packet whose value of field F_1 is in set $I(e_j)$ doesn't match r_{i+1}.
(2) $S_1 \cap I(e_j) = I(e_j)$: In this case, for a packet whose value of field F_1 is in set $I(e_j)$, it may match one of the first i rules, and it also may match rule r_{i+1}. So we append the rule $(F_2 \in S_2) \wedge \cdots \wedge (F_d \in S_d) \rightarrow \langle decision \rangle$ to the subgraph rooted at the node that e_j points to.
(3) $S_1 \cap I(e_j) \neq \emptyset$ and $S_1 \cap I(e_j) \neq I(e_j)$: In this case, we split edge e into two edges: e' with label $I(e_j) - S_1$ and e'' with label $I(e_j) \cap S_1$. Then we make two copies of the subgraph rooted at the node that e_j points to, and let e' and e'' point to one copy each. We then deal with e' by the first case, and e'' by the second case.

In the following pseudocode of the construction algorithm, we use $e.t$ to denote the (target) node that the edge e points to.

Construction Algorithm
Input : A firewall f of a sequence of rules $\langle r_1, \cdots, r_n \rangle$
Output : An FDD f' such that f and f' are equivalent
Steps:
1. build a decision path with root v from rule r_1;
2. **for** $i := 2$ **to** n **do** APPEND(v, r_i);
End

APPEND(v, $(F_m \in S_m) \wedge \cdots \wedge (F_d \in S_d) \rightarrow \langle decision \rangle$)
/*$F(v) = F_m$ and $E(v) = \{e_1, \cdots, e_k\}$*/
1. **if** ($S_m - (I(e_1) \cup \cdots \cup I(e_k))$) $\neq \emptyset$ **then**
    (a) add an outgoing edge e_{k+1} with label
        $S_m - (I(e_1) \cup \cdots \cup I(e_k))$ to v;
    (b) build a decision path from rule
        $(F_{m+1} \in S_{m+1}) \wedge \cdots \wedge (F_d \in S_d) \rightarrow \langle decision \rangle$,
        and make e_{k+1} point to the first node in this path;
2. **if** $m < d$ **then**
    for $j := 1$ **to** k **do**
        if $I(e_j) \subseteq S_m$ **then**
            APPEND($e_j.t$, $(F_{m+1} \in S_{m+1}) \wedge \cdots \wedge (F_d \in S_d)$
                                    $\rightarrow \langle decision \rangle$);
        else if $I(e_j) \cap S_m \neq \emptyset$ **then**
            (a) add one outgoing edge e to v,
                and label e with $I(e_j) \cap S_m$;
            (b) make a copy of the subgraph rooted at $e_j.t$,
                and make e points to the root of the copy;
            (a) replace the label of e_j by $I(e_j) - S_m$;
            (d) APPEND($e.t$, $(F_{m+1} \in S_{m+1}) \wedge \cdots \wedge (F_d \in S_d)$
                                    $\rightarrow \langle decision \rangle$);

As an example, consider the sequence of rules in Figure 3.4. Figure 3.5 shows the partial FDD that we construct from the first rule, and the partial FDD after we append the second rule. The FDD after we append the third rule is shown in Figure 3.6.

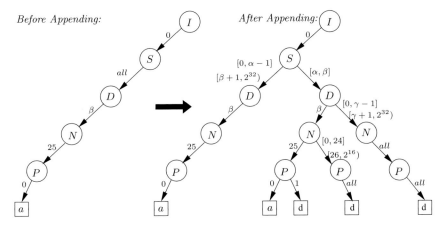

Fig. 3.5 Appending rule $(I \in \{0\}) \wedge (S \in [\alpha, \beta]) \wedge (D \in all) \wedge (N \in all) \wedge (P \in all) \rightarrow d$

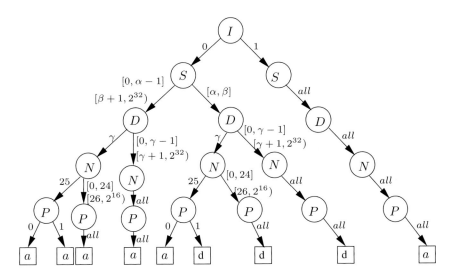

Fig. 3.6 The FDD constructed from Figure 3.4

3.2 Shaping Algorithm

In this section we discuss how to transform two ordered, but not semi-isomorphic FDDs f_a and f_b to two semi-isomorphic FDDs f'_a and f'_b such that f_a is equivalent to f'_a, and f_b is equivalent to f'_b. We define ordered

FDDs and semi-isomorphic FDDs as follows.

Definition 3.2.1 (Ordered FDDs). *Let $\prec$ be the total order over the packet fields $F_1, \cdots, F_d$ where $F_1 \prec \cdots \prec F_d$ holds. An FDD is ordered iff for each decision path $(v_1 e_1 \cdots v_k e_k v_{k+1})$, we have $F(v_1) \prec \cdots \prec F(v_k)$.* □

From this definition, the FDDs constructed by the construction algorithm in Section 3.1 are ordered. Therefore, if a firewall f designed by a team is a non-ordered FDD f, we first generate a sequence of rules that consists of all the rules in $f.rules$, where $f.rules$ is the set of all the rules defined by the decision paths of f; second, we construct an equivalent ordered FDD f' from the sequence of rules. Then use f', instead of f, to compare with other firewalls.

Informally, two FDDs are semi-isomorphic if their graphs are isomorphic, the labels of their corresponding nonterminal nodes match, and the labels of their corresponding edges match. In other words, only the labels of their terminal nodes may differ. Formally:

Definition 3.2.2 (Semi-isomorphic FDDs). *Two FDDs f_a and f_b are semi-isomorphic iff there exists a one-to-one mapping σ from the nodes of f_a onto the nodes of f_b, such that the following two conditions hold:*

(1) For any node v in f_a, either both v and $\sigma(v)$ are nonterminal nodes with the same label, or both of them are terminal nodes;

(2) For each edge e in f_a, where e is from a node v_1 to a node v_2, there is an edge e' from $\sigma(v_1)$ to $\sigma(v_2)$ in f_b, and the two edges e and e' have the same label. □

The algorithm for transforming two ordered FDDs to two semi-isomorphic FDDs uses the following three basic operations. (Note that none of these operations changes the semantics of the FDDs.)

(1) Node Insertion: If along all the decision paths containing a node v, there is no node that is labelled with a field F, then we can insert a node v' labelled F above v as follows: make all incoming edges of v point to v', create one edge from v' to v, and label this edge with the domain of F.

(2) Edge Splitting: For an edge e from v_1 to v_2, if $I(e) = S_1 \cup S_2$, where neither S_1 nor S_2 is empty, then we can split e into two edges as follows: replace e by two edges from v_1 to v_2, label one edge with S_1 and label the other with S_2.

(3) Subgraph Replication: If a node v has m $(m \geq 2)$ incoming edges, we can make m copies of the subgraph rooted at v, and make each incoming edge of v point to the root of one distinct copy.

3.2.1 FDD Simplifying

Before applying the shaping algorithm, presented below, to two ordered FDDs, we need to transform each of them to an equivalent simple FDD. A simple FDD is defined as follows:

Definition 3.2.3 (Simple FDDs). *An FDD is simple iff each node in the FDD has at most one incoming edge and each edge in the FDD is labelled with a single interval.* □

It is straightforward that the two operations of edge splitting and subgraph replication can be applied repetitively to an FDD in order to make this FDD simple. Note that the graph of a simple FDD is an outgoing directed tree. In other words, each node in a simple FDD, except the root, has only one parent node, and has only one incoming edge (from the parent node).

3.2.2 Node Shaping

Next, we introduce the procedure for transforming two shapable nodes to two semi-isomorphic nodes, which is the basic building block in the shaping algorithm for transforming two ordered FDDs to two semi-isomorphic FDDs. Shapable nodes and semi-isomorphic nodes are defined as follows.

Definition 3.2.4 (Shapable Nodes). *Let f_a and f_b be two ordered simple FDDs, v_a be a node in f_a and v_b be a node in f_b. Nodes v_a and v_b are shapable iff one of the following two conditions holds:*

(1) Both v_a and v_b have no parents, i.e., they are the roots of their respective FDDs;
(2) Both v_a and v_b have parents, their parents have the same label, and their incoming edges have the same label. □

For example, the two nodes labelled F_1 in Figure 3.7 are shapable since they have no parents.

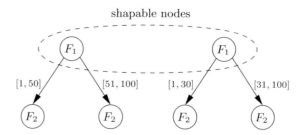

Fig. 3.7   Two shapable nodes in two FDDs

Definition 3.2.5 (Semi-isomorphic Nodes). *Let f_a and f_b be two ordered simple FDDs, v_a be a node in f_a and v_b be a node in f_b. The two nodes v_a and v_b are semi-isomorphic iff one of the following two conditions holds:*

(1) Both v_a and v_b are terminal nodes;
(2) Both v_a and v_b are nonterminal nodes with the same label and there exists a one-to-one mapping σ from the children of v_a to the children of v_b such that for each child v of v_a, v and $\sigma(v)$ are shapable. □

The algorithm for making two shapable nodes v_a and v_b semi-isomorphic consists of two steps:

(1) Step I: This step is skipped if v_a and v_b have the same label, or both of them are terminal nodes. Otherwise, without loss of generality, assume $F(v_a) \prec F(v_b)$. It is straightforward to show that in this case along all the decision paths containing node v_b, no node is labelled $F(v_a)$. Therefore, we can create a new node v_b' with label $F(v_a)$, create a new edge with label $D(F(v_a))$ from v_b' to v_b, and make all incoming edges of v_b point to v_b'. Now v_a have the same label as v_b'. (Recall that this node insertion operation leaves the semantics of the FDD unchanged.)
(2) Step II: From the previous step, we can assume that v_a and v_b have the same label. In the current step, we use the two operations of edge splitting and subgraph replication to build a one-to-one correspondence from the children of v_a to the children of v_b such that each child of v_a and its corresponding child of v_b are shapable.
Suppose $D(F(v_a)) = D(F(v_b)) = [a, b]$. We know that each outgoing edge of v_a or v_b is labelled with a single interval. Suppose v_a has m outgoing edges $\{e_1, \cdots, e_m\}$, where $I(e_i) = [a_i, b_i]$, $a_1 = a$, $b_m = b$, and

every $a_{i+1} = b_i + 1$. Also suppose v_b has n outgoing edges $\{e'_1, \cdots, e'_n\}$, where $I(e'_i) = [a'_i, b'_i]$, $a'_1 = a$, $b'_n = b$, and every $a'_{i+1} = b'_i + 1$. Comparing edge e_1, whose label is $[a, b_1]$, and e'_1, whose label is $[a, b'_1]$, we have the following two cases: (1) $b_1 = b'_1$: In this case $I(e_1) = I(e'_1)$, therefore, node $e_1.t$ and node $e'_1.t$ are shapable. (Recall that we use $e.t$ to denote the node that edge e points to.) Then we can continue to compare e_2 and e'_2 since both $I(e_2)$ and $I(e'_2)$ begin with $b_1 + 1$. (2) $b_1 \neq b'_1$: Without loss of generality, we assume $b_1 < b'_1$. In this case, we split e'_1 into two edges e and e', where e is labelled $[a, b_1]$ and e' is labelled $[b_1 + 1, b'_1]$. Then we make two copies of the subgraph rooted at $e'_1.t$ and let e and e' point to one copy each. Thus $I(e_1) = I(e)$ and the two nodes, $e_1.t$ and $e.t$ are shapable. Then we can continue to compare the two edges e_2 and e' since both $I(e_2)$ and $I(e')$ begin with $b_1 + 1$. The above process continues until we reach the last outgoing edge of v_a and the last outgoing edge of v_b. Note that each time that we compare an outgoing edge of v_a and an outgoing edge of v_b, the two intervals labelled on the two edges begin with the same value. Therefore, the last two edges that we compare must have the same label because they both ends with b. In other words, this edge splitting and subgraph replication process will terminate. When it terminates, v_a and v_b become semi-isomorphic.

In the following pseudocode for making two shapable nodes in two ordered simple FDDs semi-isomorphic, we use $I(e) < I(e')$ to indicate that every integer in $I(e)$ is less than every integer in $I(e')$.

Procedure Node_Shaping(f_a, f_b, v_a, v_b **)**
Input : Two ordered simple FDDs f_a and f_b, and
     two shapable nodes v_a in f_a and v_b in f_b
Output: The two nodes v_a and v_b become semi-isomorphic, and the
     procedure returns a set S of node pairs of the form (w_a, w_b)
     where w_a is a child of v_a in f_a, w_b is a child of v_b in f_b,
     and the two nodes w_a and w_b are shapable.
Steps:
1. **if** (both v_a and v_b are terminal) **return(** $\emptyset$ **)**;
   else if $\sim$(both v_a and v_b are nonterminal and they have the same label)
   then /*Here either both v_a and v_b are nonterminal and they have different
         labels, or one node is terminal and the other is nonterminal.
         Without loss of generality, assume one of the following conditions holds:

(1) both v_a and v_b are nonterminal and $F(v_a) \prec F(v_b)$,

(2) v_a is nonterminal and v_b is terminal.*/

insert a new node with label $F(v_a)$ above v_b, and call the new node v_b;

2. let $E(v_a)$ be $\{e_{a,1}, \cdots, e_{a,m}\}$ where $I(e_{a,1}) < \cdots < I(e_{a,m})$.

let $E(v_b)$ be $\{e_{b,1}, \cdots, e_{b,n}\}$ where $I(e_{b,1}) < \cdots < I(e_{b,n})$.

3. $i := 1$; $j := 1$;

  while (($i < m$) or ($j < n$)) **do**{

    /*During this loop, the two intervals $I(e_{a,i})$ and

    $I(e_{b,j})$ always begin with the same integer.*/

    let $I(e_{a,i}) = [A, B]$ and $I(e_{b,j}) = [A, C]$, where

    $\qquad\qquad\qquad A$, B, C are three integers;

    if $B = C$ **then** $\{i := i + 1; j := j + 1; \}$

    else if $B < C$ **then**{

        (a) create an outgoing edge e of v_b,

            and label e with $[A, B]$;

        (b) make a copy of the subgraph rooted at $e_{b,j}.t$ and

            make e point to the root of the copy;

        (c) $I(e_{b,j}) := [B + 1, C]$;

        (d) $i := i + 1;\}$

    else $\{/*B > C*/$

        (a) create an outgoing edge e of v_a,

            and label e with $[A, C]$;

        (b) make a copy of the subgraph rooted at $e_{a,j}.t$ and

            make e point to the root of the copy;

        (c) $I(e_{a,i}) := [C + 1, B]$;

        (d) $j := j + 1;\}$

  }

4. /*Now v_a and v_b become semi-isomorphic.*/

  let $E(v_a) = \{e_{a,1}, \cdots, e_{a,k}\}$ where

    $I(e_{a,1}) < \cdots < I(e_{a,k})$ and $k \geq 1$;

  let $E(v_b) = \{e_{b,1}, \cdots, e_{b,k}\}$ where

    $I(e_{b,1}) < \cdots < I(e_{b,k})$ and $k \geq 1$;

  $S := \emptyset$;

  for $i = 1$ **to** k **do**

    add the pair of shapable nodes ($e_{a,i}.t$, $e_{b,i}.t$) to S;

  return(S);

End

If we apply the above node shaping procedure to the two shapable nodes labelled F_1 in Figure 3.7, we make them semi-isomorphic as shown in Figure 3.8.

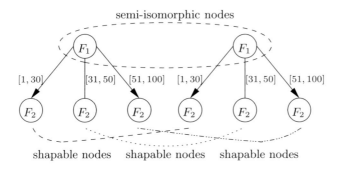

Fig. 3.8   Two semi-isomorphic nodes

3.2.3   FDD Shaping

To make two ordered FDDs f_a and f_b semi-isomorphic, at first we make f_a and f_b simple, then we make f_a and f_b semi-isomorphic as follows. Suppose we have a queue Q, which is initially empty. At first we put the pair of shapable nodes consisting of the root of f_a and the root of f_b into Q. As long as Q is not empty, we remove the head of Q, feed the two shapable nodes to the above *Node_Shaping* procedure, then put all the pairs of shapable nodes returned by the *Node_Shaping* procedure into Q. When the algorithm finishes, f_a and f_b become semi-isomorphic. The pseudocode for this shaping algorithm is as follows:

Shaping Algorithm
Input   : Two ordered FDDs f_a and f_b
Output : f_a and f_b become semi-isomorphic.
Steps:
1. make the two FDDs f_a and f_b simple;
2. $Q := \emptyset$;
3. add the shapable pair (*root of* f_a, *root of* f_b) to Q;
4. **while** $Q \neq \emptyset$ **do**{
        remove the header pair (v_a, v_b) from Q;
        $S :=$ Node_Shaping(f_a, f_b, v_a, v_b);

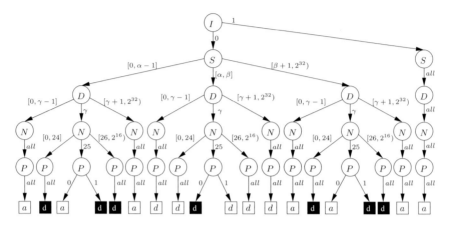

Fig. 3.9   The FDD transformed from the FDD in Figure 3.3

add every shapable pair from S into Q;

}
End

As an example, if we apply the above shaping algorithm to the two FDDs in Figure 3.3 and 3.6, we obtain two semi-isomorphic FDDs. One of those FDDs is shown in Figure 3.9, and the other one is identical to the one in Figure 3.9 with one exception: the labels of the black terminal nodes are reversed.

3.3   Comparison Algorithm

In this section, we consider how to compare two semi-isomorphic FDDs. Given two semi-isomorphic FDDs f_a and f_b with a one-to-one mapping σ, each decision path $(v_1 e_1 \cdots v_k e_k v_{k+1})$ in f_a has a corresponding decision path $(\sigma(v_1)\sigma(e_1)\cdots\sigma(v_k)\sigma(e_k)\sigma(v_{k+1}))$ in f_b. Similarly, each rule $(F(v_1) \in I(e_1)) \wedge \cdots \wedge (F(v_k) \in I(e_k)) \rightarrow F(v_{k+1})$ in $f_a.rules$ has a corresponding rule $(F(\sigma(v_1)) \in I(\sigma(e_1))) \wedge \cdots \wedge (F(\sigma(v_k)) \in I(\sigma(e_k))) \rightarrow F(\sigma(v_{k+1}))$ in $f_b.rules$. Note that $F(v_i) = F(\sigma(v_i))$ and $I(e_i) = I(\sigma(e_i))$ for each i where $1 \leq i \leq k$. Therefore, for each rule $(F(v_1) \in I(e_1)) \wedge \cdots \wedge (F(v_k) \in I(e_k)) \rightarrow F(v_{k+1})$ in $f_a.rules$, the corresponding rule in $f_b.rules$ is $(F(v_1) \in I(e_1)) \wedge \cdots \wedge (F(v_k) \in I(e_k)) \rightarrow F(\sigma(v_{k+1}))$. Each of these two rules is called the *companion* of the other. This companionship implies a one-to-one mapping from the rules defined by the decision paths in f_a to the rules defined by the decision paths in f_b. Note that for each rule and its companion, either they are identical, or they have the same predicate but different decisions. Therefore, $f_a.rules - f_b.rules$ is the set of all the rules in $f_a.rules$ that have different decisions from their companions. Similarly for $f_b.rules - f_a.rules$. Note that the set of all the companions of the rules in $f_a.rules - f_b.rules$ is $f_b.rules - f_a.rules$; and similarly the set of all the companions of the rules in $f_b.rules - f_a.rules$ is $f_a.rules - f_b.rules$. Since these two sets manifest the discrepancies between the two FDDs, the two design teams can investigate them to resolve the discrepancies.

Let f_a be the FDD in Figure 3.9, and let f_b be the FDD that is identical to f_a with one exception: the labels of the black terminal nodes are reversed. Here f_a is equivalent to the firewall in Figure 3.3 designed by Team A, and f_b is equivalent to the firewall in Figure 3.4 designed by Team B. By comparing f_a and f_b, We discover the following discrepancies between the two firewalls designed by Team A and Team B:

(1) $(I \in \{0\}) \wedge (S \in [\alpha, \beta]) \wedge (D \in \{\gamma\}) \wedge (N \in \{25\}) \wedge (P \in \{0\}) \to d$ in f_a / a in f_b
Question to investigate: Should we allow the computers from the malicious domain send email to the mail server? Team A says no, while Team B says yes.

(2) $(I \in \{0\}) \wedge (S \in [0, \alpha - 1] \cup [\beta + 1, 2^{32})) \wedge (D \in \{\gamma\}) \wedge (N \in \{25\}) \wedge (P \in \{1\}) \wedge \to d$ in f_a / a in f_b
Question to investigate: Should we allow UDP packets sent from the hosts who are not in the malicious domain to the mail server? Team A says no, while Team B says yes.

(3) $(I \in \{0\}) \wedge (S \in [0, \alpha - 1] \cup [\beta + 1, 2^{32})) \wedge (D \in \{\gamma\}) \wedge (N \in [0, 24] \cup [26, 2^{16}) \wedge (P \in all) \wedge \to d$ in f_a / a in f_b
Question to investigate: Should we allow the packets with a port number other than 25 be sent from the hosts who are not in the malicious domain to the mail server? Team A says no, while Team B says yes.

3.4 Experimental Results

In this chapter we presented three algorithms, a construction algorithm, a shaping algorithm and a comparison algorithm. These three algorithms can be used to detect all discrepancies between two given firewalls. In this section, we evaluate the efficiency of each of these three algorithms.

The construction algorithm is evaluated by the average time for constructing an FDD from a sequence of rules. The shaping algorithm is evaluated by the average time for shaping two FDDs where each is an FDD constructed from a sequence rules that we generate independently. The comparison algorithm is measured by the average time for detecting all the discrepancies between two semi-isomorphic FDDs that we get from the shaping algorithm. In the absence of publicly available firewalls, we create synthetic firewalls based on the characteristics of real-life packet classifiers discovered in [Baboescu *et al.* (2003); Gupta (2000)]. Each rule has the following five fields: interface, source IP address, destination IP address, destination port number and protocol type.

The programs are implemented in SUN Java JDK 1.4. The experiments were carried out on a SunBlade 2000 machine running Solaris 9 with 1Ghz CPU and 1 GB memory. Figure 3.10 shows the average execution times for the construction algorithm, for the shaping algorithm, and for the comparison algorithm versus the total number of rules. We also measured the average total time for detecting all the discrepancies between two sequences of rules, which includes the time for constructing two ordered FDDs from two sequences of rules, shaping the two ordered FDDs to be semi-isomorphic, and comparing the two semi-isomorphic FDDs. From this figure, we see that it takes less than 5 seconds to detect all the discrepancies between two sequences of 3000 rules. In fact, it is very unlikely that a firewall can have this many rules (see the characteristics of real-life packet classifiers in [Baboescu *et al.* (2003); Gupta (2000)]). Clearly the efficiency of the three algorithms make them attractive to be used in practice for supporting the diverse firewall design method.

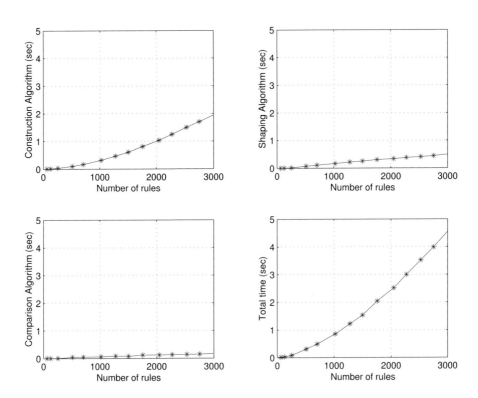

Fig. 3.10   Experimental Results

Chapter 4

Stateful Firewall Model

A firewall is placed at the point of entry between a private network and the outside Internet so that all incoming and outgoing packets have to pass through it. The function of a firewall is to map each incoming or outgoing packet to one of a set of predefined decisions, such as *accept* or *discard*. Based on how a decision is made for every packet, firewalls are categorized into stateless firewalls and stateful firewalls. If a firewall decides the fate of every packet solely by examining the packet itself, then the firewall is called a *stateless firewall*. If a firewall decides the fate of some packets not only by examining the packet itself but also by examining the packets that the firewall has accepted previously, then the firewall is called a *stateful firewall*. Using a stateful firewall to protect a private network, one can achieve finer access control by tracking the communication state between the private network and the outside Internet. For example, a stateful firewall can refuse to accept any packet from a remote host to a local host unless the local host has previously sent a packet to the remote host.

Although a variety of stateful firewall products have been available and deployed on the Internet for some time, such as Cisco PIX Firewalls, Cisco Reflexive ACLs, CheckPoint FireWall-1 and Netfilter/IPTables, no model for specifying stateful firewalls exists. The lack of such a model constitutes a significant impediment for further development of stateful firewall technologies. First, without a model, it is difficult to conduct research on stateful firewalls. This explains why so little research on stateful firewalls has been done so far. In contrast, benefiting from the well-established rule based model of stateless firewalls, the research results for stateless firewalls have been numerous. People have known how to design stateless firewalls [Bartal *et al.* (1999); Guttman (1997); Gouda and Liu (2004); Liu and Gouda (2004)] and how to analyze stateless firewalls [Liu *et al.* (2004);

Al-Shaer and Hamed (2004); Mayer *et al.* (2000); Wool (2001); Kamara *et al.* (2003); Frantzen *et al.* (2001)]. But the question of how to design and analyze stateful firewalls remains unanswered. Second, because there is no specification model for stateful firewalls, in existing stateful firewall products, state tracking functionalities have been hard coded and different vendors hard code different state tracking functionalities. For example, the Cisco PIX Firewalls do not track the state for ICMP packets. Consequently, it is hard for the administrator of such a firewall to track the Ping [Postel (1981)] protocol. Last, without a specification model, it is difficult to analyze the properties of stateful firewalls. For example, it is difficult to analyze the properties of existing stateful firewalls because some of the functions of these firewalls are hard coded while others are specified by their administrators. All in all, a specification model for stateful firewalls is greatly needed.

In this chapter, we present the first stateful firewall model. In the firewall model, each firewall has a variable set called the *state* of the firewall, which is used to store some packets that the firewall has accepted previously and needs to remember in the near future. Each firewall consists of two sections: a *stateful section* and a *stateless section*. Each section consists of a sequence of rules. For every packet, the stateful section is used to check whether the state has a previous packet that may affect the fate of the current packet. To store this checking result, we assume that each packet has an additional field called the tag. The stateless section is used to decide the fate of each packet based on the information in the packet itself and its tag value.

The stateful firewall model has the following favorable properties. First, it can express a variety of state tracking functionalities. Using a set of packets to record communication state provides a great deal of flexibility in expressing state tracking functionalities since the state of a communication protocol is characterized by packets. In a sense, the stateful firewall model captures the essence of communication states. Second, because we separate a firewall into a stateful section and a stateless section, we can inherit the existing rich results in designing and analyzing stateless firewalls because a stateless section alone is in fact a full-fledged stateless firewall. Third, the model is simple, easy to use, easy to understand, and easy to implement. Last, the model is a generalization of the current stateless firewall model. Although the model is intended to specify stateful firewalls, it can also be used to specify stateless firewalls, simply by leaving the stateful section empty and keeping the state empty. This backward compatibility gives a stateful firewall product the flexibility of being specified as either a stateful firewall or a stateless firewall.

This chapter goes beyond presenting the stateful firewall model itself. A significant portion of this chapter is devoted to analyzing the properties of stateful firewalls that are specified using the model. We outline a method for verifying that a firewall is truly stateful. The method is based on three properties of firewalls: conforming, grounded, and proper. We show that if a firewall satisfies these three properties, then the firewall is truly stateful. We also discuss the implementation details of the model. To speed up membership query, we use Bloom filters to facilitate implementing and querying the set *"state"*.

The rest of this chapter proceeds as follows. In Section 4.1, we introduce the syntax and semantics of the firewall model. In Section 4.2, we give two examples of stateful firewalls that are specified using the model. In Section 4.3, we discuss how to remove packets that are no longer needed from the state of a firewall. In Section 4.4, we study the issues related to firewall states. In Section 4.5, we present a method for verifying that a firewall is truly stateful.

For simplicity, in the rest of this chapter, we use "firewall" to mean "stateful firewall" unless otherwise specified.

4.1 Firewall Model

In this section, we introduce the firewall model through an example of a simple firewall that resides on the gateway router depicted in Figure 4.1. This router has two interfaces: interface 0, which connects the router to the outside Internet, and interface 1, which connects the router to a private network.

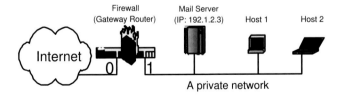

Fig. 4.1 A firewall for a private network

Stateful Section:

R_1 : $I \in \{0\} \wedge P \in \{icmp\} \wedge T \in \{pong\}$ $\wedge S = D' \wedge D = S' \wedge ID = ID'$ $\wedge$
  $SN = SN' \rightarrow tag := 1$

Stateless Section:

r_1 : $I \in \{1\} \wedge P \in \{icmp\} \wedge T \in \{ping\} \wedge tag \in all$ $\rightarrow$ *accept; insert*

r_2 : $I \in \{1\} \wedge P \in all$ $\wedge T \in all$ $\wedge tag \in all$ $\rightarrow$ *accept*

r_3 : $I \in \{0\} \wedge P \in \{icmp\} \wedge T \in \{pong\} \wedge tag \in \{1\}$ $\rightarrow$ *accept*

r_4 : $I \in \{0\} \wedge P \in \{icmp\} \wedge T \in \{pong\} \wedge tag \in \{0\}$ $\rightarrow$ *discard*

r_5 : $I \in \{0\} \wedge P \in all$ $\wedge T \in all$ $\wedge tag \in all$ $\rightarrow$ *accept*

Fig. 4.2 Tracking the Ping protocol

  This firewall tracks the Ping protocol (Packet Internet Groper Protocol) [Postel (1981)] to counter "smurf" attacks. The Ping protocol is used by a host to determine whether another host is up. When a host A wants to test whether a host B is up, A sends to B a series of ICMP (Internet Control Message Protocol) ping (i.e., echo request) packets. All of these ping packets have the same ID but different sequence numbers. When B receives from A a ping packet with ID x and sequence number y, B sends back to A a pong (i.e., echo reply) packet with the same ID x and the same sequence number y. The "smurf" attack, a type of Denial of Service attack, works as follows. An attacker sends a ping packet, whose source IP address has been forged to be the IP address of a victim host, to the broadcast address of a subnetwork. Subsequently, every host on the subnetwork will send a pong packet to the victim host.

  One way to counter "smurf" attacks for a private network is to use a firewall to discard every incoming pong packet unless the packet corresponds to a previous ping packet sent from the private network. Suppose that we want to configure the firewall in Figure 4.1 in such a fashion. When a pong packet arrives, the firewall needs to check whether it has seen the corresponding ping packet. This requires the firewall to remember the ping packets sent from the private network to the outside. In the firewall model, each firewall has a variable set called the state. The state of a firewall contains the packets that the firewall has accepted previously and needs to remember in the near future. In this firewall example, we store in the state of the firewall the ping packets that are sent from the private network to the outside Internet.

  In the firewall model, each firewall consists of two sections: a *stateful section* and a *stateless section*. The stateful section is used to check each packet against the state. The stateless section is used to decide the fate of a packet after the packet has been checked against the state. To store the checking result of the stateful section for each packet, we assume that each packet has an additional field called the *tag*. The value of the tag field of a packet is an integer, whose initial value is zero. The domain of this tag field depends on how many possible tag values that a firewall needs. In the above firewall example, when a packet arrives, if it is a pong packet and its corresponding ping packet is in the state, then the tag field of the packet is assigned 1; otherwise the tag field of the packet retains the initial value of 0. Therefore, the domain of the tag field in this example is $[0, 1]$.

We define a *packet* over the fields $F_1, \cdots, F_d$ to be a d-tuple $(p_1, \cdots, p_d)$ where each p_i is in the domain $D(F_i)$ of field F_i, and each $D(F_i)$ is an interval of nonnegative integers. For example, the domain of the source address in an IP packet is $[0, 2^{32})$.

The stateful section of a firewall consists a sequence of rules where each rule is called a *stateful rule*. A stateful rule is of the form

$$P(F_1, \cdots, F_d, F_1', \cdots, F_d', tag') \to tag := x$$

where

$P(F_1, \cdots, F_d, F_1', \cdots, F_d', tag')$ is a predicate over $F_1, \cdots, F_d, F_1', \cdots, F_d', tag'$. A packet $(p_1, \cdots, p_d)$ *matches* the above rule iff (if and only if) there exists a packet $(p_1', \cdots, p_d')$ with tag value t' in the state of the firewall such that $P(p_1, \cdots, p_d, p_1', \cdots, p_d', t')$ is true. The meaning of this stateful rule is as follows. Given a packet p such that p matches this stateful rule (but p does not match any other stateful rules listed before this rule), the tag value of this packet p is changed from its initial value 0 to the new value x.

The stateless section of a firewall also consists a sequence of rules where each rule is called a *stateless rule*. A stateless rule is of the form

$$F_1 \in S_1 \wedge \cdots \wedge F_d \in S_d \wedge tag \in S_t \to \langle decision \rangle$$

where each S_i is a nonempty subset of the domain of F_i for $0 \le i \le d$, and S_t is a nonempty subset of the domain of the tag field, and the $\langle decision \rangle$ is "*accept*", or "*accept; insert*", or "*discard*". For each i ($1 \le i \le d$), if $S_i = D(F_i)$, we can replace $F_i \in S_i$ by $F_i \in all$, or remove the conjunct $F_i \in D(F_i)$ from the rule. A packet $(p_1, \cdots, p_d)$ with tag value t *matches* the above rule iff the condition $p_1 \in S_1 \wedge \cdots \wedge p_d \in S_d \wedge t \in S_t$ holds. The meaning of this stateless rule is as follows. Given a packet p such that p matches this stateless rule (but p does not match any other stateless rules listed before this rule), the *decision* for this packet is executed. If the *decision* is "*accept*", then the packet p is allowed to proceed to its destination. If the *decision* is "*accept; insert*", then the packet p is allowed to proceed to its destination and additionally packet p (together with its tag value) is inserted into the state of the firewall. If the *decision* is "*discard*", then the packet p is discarded by the firewall.

In the firewall example in Figure 4.1, we assume that each packet has the following seven fields. For simplicity, in this chapter we assume that each packet has a field containing the identification of the network interface on which a packet arrives. Figure 4.2 shows this firewall specified using the model.

name	meaning	domain
I	Interface	$[0, 1]$
S	Source IP address	$[0, 2^{32})$
D	Destination IP address	$[0, 2^{32})$
P	Protocol Type	$\{tcp, udp, icmp\}$
T	echo packet type	$\{ping, pong\}$
ID	echo packet ID	$[0, 2^{16})$
SN	echo packet sequence number	$[0, 2^{16})$

In this firewall example, the stateful section consists of one rule: $I \in \{0\} \wedge P \in \{icmp\} \wedge T \in \{pong\} \wedge S = D' \wedge D = S' \wedge ID = ID' \wedge SN = SN' \rightarrow tag := 1$. The meaning of this rule is as follows: if a packet p is an incoming pong packet (indicated by $I \in \{0\} \wedge P \in \{icmp\} \wedge T \in \{pong\}$), and there exists a packet p' in the state such that the following four conditions hold:

(1) the source address of p equals the destination address of p' (denoted $S = D'$),
(2) the destination address of p equals the source address of p' (denoted $D = S'$),
(3) the ID of p equals the ID of p' (denoted $ID = ID'$),
(4) the sequence number of p equals the sequence number of p' (denoted $SN = SN'$),

then the tag field of packet p is assigned 1; otherwise the tag field of packet p retains its initial value 0. In this firewall example, the stateless section consists of five rules whose function is to map every packet with a certain tag value to one of predefined decisions. Note that the meaning of the rule r_1 is as follows. Given a packet over the seven fields (namely I, S, D, P, T, ID, SN), if the packet matches rule r_1, then the firewall allows this packet to proceed to its destination and additionally the packet (which is a tuple over the seven fields) together with its tag value is inserted into the state of the firewall.

Note that when a firewall inserts a packet $(p_1, \cdots, p_d)$ with a tag value into the state of the firewall, the firewall may not need to insert all the d fields of the packet. For example, considering the above firewall example in Figure 4.2, its stateful section consists of one rule $I \in \{0\} \wedge P \in \{icmp\} \wedge T \in \{pong\} \wedge S = D' \wedge D = S' \wedge ID = ID' \wedge SN = SN' \rightarrow tag := 1$. This rule only examines four fields of the packets in the state: S, D, ID and SN. Therefore, instead of inserting a packet of all the seven fields (namely I, S, D, P, T, ID, SN) together with the tag value of the packet into the state, we only need to insert a tuple over the above four fields of S, D, ID and SN.

Two stateless rules *conflict* iff there exists at least one packet that matches both rules and the two rules have different decisions. For example, rule r_1 and rule r_2 in the stateless section of the firewall in Figure 4.2 conflict. Two stateful rules *conflict* iff in a reachable state of the firewall there exists at least one packet that matches both rules and the two rules have different decisions. In the firewall model, for both the stateful section and the stateless section, we follow the convention that stateless firewalls use to resolve conflicts: a packet is mapped to the decision of the first rule that the packet matches.

A set of rules is *comprehensive* iff for any packet there is at least one rule in the set that the packet matches. The set of all the rules in the stateless section of a firewall must be comprehensive because each packet needs to be mapped to a decision. Note that the set of all the rules in the stateful section of a firewall does not need to be comprehensive. This is because the function of a stateful section is to assign nonzero values to the tag fields of some packets, but not all packets.

Given a packet to a firewall specified using the model, Figure 4.3 describes how the firewall processes this packet.

By separating a firewall into a stateful section and a stateless section, we can inherit existing research results of stateless firewalls because a stateless section alone is in fact a full-fledged stateless firewall. For example, existing stateless firewall design methods [Bartal *et al.* (1999); Guttman (1997); Gouda and Liu (2004); Liu and Gouda (2004)], and stateless firewall analysis methods [Liu *et al.* (2004); Al-Shaer and Hamed (2004); Mayer *et al.* (2000); Wool (2001); Kamara *et al.* (2003); Frantzen *et al.* (2001)], are still applicable to the design and analysis of a stateless section. In addition, existing packet classification algorithms for stateless firewalls can still be used to map a packet with a certain tag value to the first rule that the packet matches in the stateless section.

Step 1. **Checking in the stateful section**:
    If $P(F_1, \cdots, F_d, F'_1, \cdots, F'_d, tag') \to tag := x$
       is the first stateful rule that the given packet matches
    then the tag of the packet is assigned value x;
    else the tag of the packet retains value 0.

Step 2. **Checking in the stateless section**:
    If $F_1 \in S_1 \wedge \cdots \wedge F_d \in S_d \wedge tag \in S_t \to \langle decision \rangle$
    is the first stateless rule that the given packet matches
    then the $\langle decision \rangle$ is executed for the packet.

Fig. 4.3   Processing a given packet

4.2 Firewall Examples

In this section, we show two more examples of stateful firewalls.

4.2.1 Example I: Tracking Outgoing Packets

Suppose that the requirements for the firewall in Figure 4.1 are as follows:

(1) Any packet from the outside malicious domain 192.168.0.0/16 should be discarded.
(2) The mail server, with IP address 192.1.2.3, should be able to send and receive emails, but non-email traffic is not allowed to proceed to the mail server.
(3) Any packet from a remote host to a local host, which is not the mail server, is discarded unless the local host has already sent a packet to the remote host earlier. In other words, the communication between a local host and a remote host can only be initiated by the local host.

In this example, we assume that each packet has six fields. Four of them have been discussed earlier: I (interface), S (source IP address), D (destination IP address), and P (protocol type). The remaining two are as follows:

name	meaning	domain
SP	Source Port	$[0, 2^{16})$
DP	Destination Port	$[0, 2^{16})$

Figure 4.4 shows the specification of this firewall. Its stateful section consists of one rule $I \in \{0\} \wedge S = D' \wedge D = S' \wedge SP = DP' \wedge DP = SP' \wedge P = P' \rightarrow tag := 1$. The meaning of this rule is as follows: if a packet p is an incoming packet (denoted $I \in \{0\}$), and there exists a packet p' in the state such that the following five conditions hold:

(1) the source address of p equals the destination address of p' (denoted $S = D'$),

(2) the destination address of p equals the source address of p' (denoted $D = S'$),

(3) the source port number of p equals the destination port number of p' (denoted $SP = DP'$),

(4) the destination port number of p equals the source port number of p' (denoted $DP = SP'$),

(5) the protocol type of p equals that of p' (denoted $P = P'$),

then the tag field of packet p is assigned 1; otherwise the tag field of packet p retains value 0.

The stateless section of this firewall consists of seven rules from r_1 to r_7. Note that the meaning of rule r_2 is as follows. Any outgoing packet from a local host other than the mail server is allowed to proceed to its destination, and additionally this packet, which is a tuple of the six fields (namely I, S, D, P, SP, DP), together with its tag value, is inserted into the state of the firewall. Since the stateful section of this firewall only examines the five fields (namely S, D, P, SP, and DP) of the packets in the state of this firewall, we only need to insert these five fields of a packet into the state.

4.2.2 *Example II: Tracking FTP Ptotocol*

In this section, we show an example of a firewall that tracks the FTP protocol. File Transfer Protocol (FTP) [Postel and Reynolds (1985)] is an application protocol that is used to transfer files between two hosts. We assume that the firewall in Figure 4.1 allows any local host to initiate an FTP connection to a remote host, but any remote host cannot initiate an FTP connection to a local host. For simplicity, we assume that non-FTP traffic is discarded.

What complicates the tracking of FTP is its dual-connection feature. FTP uses two TCP connections to transfer files between two hosts: a control connection and a data connection. When a client wants to connect to a re-

Stateful Section:

$R_1 : I \in \{0\} \wedge S = D' \wedge D = S' \wedge SP = DP' \wedge DP = SP' \wedge P = P'$ $\rightarrow tag := 1$

Stateless Section:

$r_1 : I \in \{1\} \wedge S \in \{192.1.2.3\} \wedge D \in all \wedge DP \in all \wedge P \in all \ \wedge \ tag \in \ all$
$\rightarrow accept$

$r_2 : I \in \{1\} \wedge S \in all \qquad \wedge D \in all \wedge DP \in all \wedge P \in all \wedge tag \in all$
$\rightarrow accept;$
$insert$

$r_3 : I \in \{0\} \wedge S \in [192.168.0.0, 192.168.255.255] \wedge D \in all \wedge DP \in all \wedge$
$\quad P \in all \wedge tag \in all$ $\rightarrow discard$

$r_4 : I \in \{0\} \wedge S \in all \wedge D \in \{192.1.2.3\} \wedge DP \in \{25\} \wedge P \in \{tcp\} \wedge tag \in all$
$\rightarrow accept$

$r_5 : I \in \{0\} \wedge S \in all \wedge D \in \{192.1.2.3\} \wedge DP \in all \wedge P \in all \wedge tag \in all$
$\rightarrow discard$

$r_6 : I \in \{0\} \wedge S \in all \wedge D \in all \wedge DP \in all \wedge P \in all \wedge tag \in \{1\}$ $\rightarrow accept$
$r_7 : I \in \{0\} \wedge S \in all \wedge D \in all \wedge DP \in all \wedge P \in all \wedge tag \in \{0\}$ $\rightarrow discard$

Fig. 4.4   Tracking outgoing packets

mote FTP server, the client uses one of its available port numbers, say x, to connect to the server on the well-known port 21. This connection, between the client's port x and the server's port 21, is called the control connection. FTP uses the control connection to transfer FTP commands such as CWD (change working directory) and PORT (specify the port number that the client will use for the data connection). After this control connection is built between the client and the server, the client sends a PORT command with a value y, where y is an available port on the client, to the server via this control connection. After this PORT command is received, the server uses its well-known port 20 to connect back to the port y of the client. This connection, between the client's port y and the server's port 20, is called the data connection. Note that the control connection is initiated by the FTP client and the data connection is initiated by the FTP server. This dual-connection feature of the FTP protocol is illustrated in Figure 4.5.

This firewall is specified in Figure 4.6. In this example, we assume that each packet has eight fields. Six of them have been discussed earlier: I (interface), S (source IP address), D (destination IP address), P (protocol type), SP (source port) and DP (destination port). The remaining two are as follows:

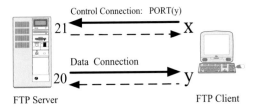

Fig. 4.5   FTP Ptotocol

name	meaning	domain
T	Application Type	$[0, 1]$
A	Application Data	$[0, 2^{16})$

For a packet, if the value of its field T is 1, then the value of its field A is the port number of a port command; otherwise field A contains another FTP control command.

Stateful Section:

$R_1 : I \in \{0\} \wedge SP \in \{21\} \wedge P \in \{tcp\} \wedge S = D' \wedge D = S' \wedge DP = SP' \wedge$
$\quad DP' \in \{21\} \qquad\qquad\qquad\qquad\qquad\qquad\qquad\qquad \rightarrow tag := 1$

$R_2 : I \in \{0\} \wedge SP \in \{20\} \wedge P \in \{tcp\} \wedge S = D' \wedge D = S' \wedge T' = 1 \wedge$
$\quad DP = A' \wedge DP' \in \{21\} \qquad\qquad\qquad\qquad\qquad \rightarrow tag := 1$

$R_3 : I \in \{1\} \wedge DP \in \{20\} \wedge P \in \{tcp\} \wedge S = D' \wedge D = S' \wedge SP = DP' \wedge$
$\quad SP' \in \{20\} \qquad\qquad\qquad\qquad\qquad\qquad\qquad\qquad \rightarrow tag := 1$

Stateless Section:

$r_1 : \quad I \in \{1\} \wedge SP \in all \quad \wedge DP \in \{21\} \quad \wedge P \in \{tcp\} \wedge tag \in all \rightarrow accept;$
$\qquad\qquad\qquad\qquad\qquad\qquad\qquad\qquad\qquad\qquad\qquad\qquad insert$

$r_2 : \quad I \in \{1\} \wedge SP \in all \quad \wedge DP \in \{20\} \quad \wedge P \in \{tcp\} \wedge tag \in \{1\} \rightarrow accept$

$r_3 : \quad I \in \{1\} \wedge SP \in all \quad \wedge DP \in all \quad \wedge P \in all \quad \wedge tag \in all \rightarrow discard$

$r_4 : \quad I \in \{0\} \wedge SP \in \{20\} \wedge DP \in all \quad \wedge P \in \{tcp\} \wedge tag \in \{1\} \rightarrow accept;$
$\qquad\qquad\qquad\qquad\qquad\qquad\qquad\qquad\qquad\qquad\qquad\qquad insert$

$r_5 : \quad I \in \{0\} \wedge SP \in \{21\} \wedge DP \in all \quad \wedge P \in \{tcp\} \wedge tag \in \{1\} \rightarrow accept$

$r_6 : \quad I \in \{0\} \wedge SP \in all \quad \wedge DP \in all \quad \wedge P \in all \quad \wedge tag \in all \rightarrow discard$

Fig. 4.6   Tracking the FTP protocol

In this example, the firewall only possibly accepts the following four types of packets: outgoing TCP packets to port 21, incoming TCP packets from port 21, incoming TCP packets from port 20, and outgoing TCP packets to port 20. Next we discuss each of these four types of packets.

(1) Outgoing TCP packets to port 21: Any packet p of this type is accepted

and inserted into the state. See rule r_1 in Figure 4.6.

(2) Incoming TCP packets from port 21: A packet p of this type is accepted iff there exists a packet p' in the state such that p's source IP address equals p''s destination IP address, p's destination IP address equals p''s source IP address, p's destination port number equals p''s source port number, and p''s destination port number is 21. See the three rules r_1, R_1, and r_5 in Figure 4.6.

(3) Incoming TCP packets from port 20: A packet p of this type is accepted iff there exists a packet p' in the state such that p's source IP address equals p''s destination IP address, p's destination IP address equals p''s source IP address, p''s destination port number is 21, p' contains a PORT command and p's destination port equals the port number in this PORT command of p'. See the three rules r_1, R_2, and r_4 in Figure 4.6.

(4) Outgoing TCP packets to port 20: A packet p of this type is accepted iff there exists a packet p' in the state such that p's source IP address equals p''s destination IP address, p's destination IP address equals p''s source IP address, p's source port number equals p''s destination port number, and p''s source port number is 20. See the three rules r_4, R_3, and r_2 in Figure 4.6.

4.3 Removing Packets from Firewall State

After a packet is inserted into the state of a firewall, the packet should be removed when it is no longer needed, otherwise security could be breached. We show this point by the firewall example in Figure 4.2 that tracks the Ping protocol. Suppose a local host named A sends a ping packet to a remote host named B. According to the specification of this firewall in Figure 4.2, this ping packet is inserted into the state of this firewall. When the corresponding pong packet comes back from host B, it is accepted by the firewall because of the stored ping packet, and additionally this stored ping packet should be removed from the state of the firewall. Otherwise, an attacker could replay the pong packet for an unlimited number of times and each of the replayed pong packets would be incorrectly allowed to proceed to the victim host A.

A new command, "*remove*", is used to remove the packets that are no longer needed from the state of a firewall. Therefore, there are two more possible decisions that a stateless rule may use: "*accept; remove*" and "*accept*; *insert*; *remove*", in addition to the three decisions (namely "*accept*", "*accept*; *insert*", and "*discard*") that we have seen earlier. The meaning of a stateless rule with decision "*accept*; *remove*" is as follows. Given a packet p, if p matches this rule (but p does not match any stateless rule listed before this rule), then p is accepted. Moreover, if the state has a packet p' such that p satisfies the predicate of the first stateful rule that p matches using p', then packet p' is removed from the state. Similarly for the meaning of a rule with decision "*accept*; *insert*; *remove*". Consider the example of the firewall in Figure 4.2 that tracks the Ping protocol. When a ping packet is sent from a local host to a remote host, the ping packet is inserted into the state of the firewall by the stateless rule $r_1 : I \in \{1\} \wedge P \in \{icmp\} \wedge T \in \{ping\} \wedge tag \in all \to accept$; *insert*. When the corresponding pong packet comes back from the remote host, it is accepted by the stateless rule r_3 and it should also trigger the removal of the stored ping packet. Therefore, a "*remove*" command should be added to rule r_3. In other words, rule r_3 should be $I \in \{0\} \wedge P \in \{icmp\} \wedge T \in \{pong\} \wedge tag \in \{1\} \to accept$; *remove*.

Usually the packet that *initiates* the "conversation" between two hosts is stored in the state of a firewall, and the packet that *terminates* the "conversation" triggers the removal of the stored packet. Examples of the packets that can initiate a conversation are ping packets and TCP SYN packets. Examples of the packets that can terminate a conversation are pong packets and TCP FIN packets.

To remove the packets that are no longer needed in the state of a firewall, we cannot only rely on some packets to trigger the removal for two reasons. First, these triggering packets may get lost on their way. Second, the processes that are supposed to send triggering packets may abnormally terminate before sending out the triggering packets. In either case, the packets that should be removed still remain in the state. To deal with these two cases, when a packet is inserted into the state of a firewall, it is assigned a TTL (Time To Live) value. The TTL value of every packet in the state decreases as time goes by. When the TTL value of a packet expires, the packet is automatically removed from the state.

Different packets may need different TTL values. Therefore, the "*insert*" command has a parameter t, which is the TTL value for the packet to be inserted into the state of a firewall. The meaning of a stateless rule with decision "*accept*; *insert*(t)" is as follows. Given a packet p such that p matches this rule (but p does not match any stateless rule listed before this rule), provided that p is not an element of the state, then p is inserted into the state with TTL value t. On the other hand, if p already exists in the state, then the TTL value of p in the state is reassigned the value t.

Figure 4.7 shows the complete firewall for tracking the Ping protocol after we incorporate the TTL extension to the *"insert"* command in rule r_1 and add the *"remove"* command to rule r_3. In this example, the TTL value in the *"insert"* command is 10 seconds.

Stateful Section:
$R_1 : I \in \{0\} \wedge P \in \{icmp\} \wedge T \in \{pong\} \ \wedge S = D' \wedge D = S' \wedge ID = ID' \wedge$
$\qquad SN = SN' \to tag := 1$

Stateless Section:
$r_1 : \ I \in \{1\} \wedge P \in \{icmp\} \wedge T \in \{ping\} \wedge tag \in all \ \to accept; \ insert(10)$
$r_2 : \ I \in \{1\} \wedge P \in all \qquad \wedge T \in all \qquad \wedge tag \in all \ \to accept$
$r_3 : \ I \in \{0\} \wedge P \in \{icmp\} \wedge T \in \{pong\} \wedge tag \in \{1\} \ \to accept; \ remove$
$r_4 : \ I \in \{0\} \wedge P \in \{icmp\} \wedge T \in \{pong\} \wedge tag \in \{0\} \ \to discard$
$r_5 : \ I \in \{0\} \wedge P \in all \qquad \wedge T \in all \qquad \wedge tag \in all \ \to accept$

Fig. 4.7   Tracking the Ping protocol (with packets removal)

4.4   Firewall States

Recall that each firewall has a variable set named the state of the firewall. Initially, the state of a firewall is empty. The transition between two states of a firewall is illustrated in Figure 4.8.

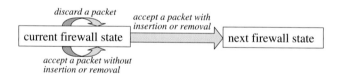

Fig. 4.8   Firewall state transition

A *history* of a firewall is a finite sequence $S.1, p.1, S.2, p.2, \cdots, S.n$ such that the following three conditions hold.

i. Each $S.i$ is a state of the firewall. Note that $S.1$ is the initial state of the firewall, which is an empty set.

ii. Each $p.i$ is a packet.

iii. For every i $(1 \le i < n)$, if the firewall is in state $S.i$ and receives packet $p.i$, then the firewall accepts $p.i$ and the state of the firewall becomes $S.(i+1)$.

Note that in a firewall history, $S.1, p.1, S.2, p.2, \cdots, S.n$, for every i $(1 \le i < n)$, we have

$$\begin{cases} S.i \ne S.(i+1) \text{ if in state } S.i, \ p.i \text{ is accepted, and} \\ \qquad\qquad p.i \text{ is inserted into the state or } p.i \\ \qquad\qquad \text{triggers the removal of an packet;} \\ S.i = S.(i+1) \text{ otherwise} \end{cases}$$

A state of a firewall is called a *reachable state* iff the state is in a history of the firewall.

4.4.1 *Truly Stateful and Truly Stateless Firewalls*

Before we define truly stateful firewalls, we first define two important concepts associated with each firewall: the accepted set and the acceptable set.

A packet is called an *accepted packet* of a firewall iff the packet can be accepted in every reachable state of the firewall. The set of all accepted packets of a firewall is called the *accepted set* of the firewall. For a firewall f, we use $f.a$ to denote its accepted set.

A packet is called an *acceptable packet* of a firewall iff the packet can be accepted in some (possibly every) reachable state of the firewall. The set of all acceptable packets of a firewall is called the *acceptable set* of the firewall. For a firewall f, we use $f.b$ to denote its acceptable set.

Note that a stateless firewall can also be specified using the model. When we specify a stateless firewall, we leave the stateful section empty and specify no "insert" command in any rule in the stateless section. In this case, the state of the firewall remains empty and the firewall is therefore stateless. For a stateless firewall f, we use $f.a$ to denote the set of all accepted packets of f and use $f.b$ to denote the set of all acceptable packets of f. From the definition of stateful firewalls and stateless firewalls, we have the following theorem:

Theorem 4.4.1. Let f be a firewall.

i. $f.a$ is a subset of $f.b$ $(f.a \subseteq f.b)$
ii. If f is stateless, then $f.a = f.b$.

A firewall f is *truly stateful* iff $f.a$ is a proper subset of $f.b$; i.e., $f.a \subset f.b$. A firewall f is *truly stateless* iff $f.a = f.b$. Clearly, a stateless firewall is truly stateless, but a stateful firewall can either be truly stateful or be truly stateless. A stateful firewall that is truly stateless can be simplified, without changing its function, by making its stateful section empty and removing the "insert" command from every rule in its stateless section.

As an example, consider the firewall in Figure 4.9(a). This firewall accepts each packet where $S \in \{0\}$ and $D \in \{1\}$ in each reachable state, and discards all other packets in each reachable state. Thus, this firewall is truly stateless (although it is syntactically stateful). Therefore, this firewall can be simplified as shown in Figure 4.9(b).

Stateful Section:
  $R_1 : S = D' \wedge D = S' \rightarrow tag := 1$
Stateless Section:
  $r_1 : S \in \{0\} \wedge D \in \{1\} \wedge tag \in all \rightarrow accept; insert$
  $r_2 : S \in all \ \wedge D \in all \ \wedge tag \in all \rightarrow discard$

(a)

Stateful Section:
Stateless Section:
  $r_1 : S \in \{0\} \wedge D \in \{1\} \wedge tag \in all \rightarrow accept$
  $r_2 : S \in all \ \wedge D \in all \ \wedge tag \in all \rightarrow discard$

(b)

Fig. 4.9   A truly stateless firewall and its simplified version

---

4.4.2   *Stateless Derivatives*

It is important that if a firewall designer designs a stateful firewall f, then he should verify that f is truly stateful. This is because if f is truly stateless, then f can be simplified into a stateless firewall. In this section, we identify a sufficient condition for verifying that a firewall is truly stateful. But first we introduce the concept of a stateless derivative of a firewall.

The *stateless derivative* of a firewall f is the firewall obtained after making the stateful section of f empty and removing the "insert" command from every rule in the stateless section of f. For example, Figure 4.9(b) shows the stateless derivative of the firewall in Figure 4.9(a).

The relationship between a firewall and its stateless derivative is stated in the following theorem.

Theorem 4.4.2. Let f be a firewall and g be its stateless derivative,

 i. $f.a \subseteq g.a$
 ii. $g.a = g.b$
iii. $g.b \subseteq f.b$

Proof of Theorem 4.4.2:
Proof of i: This assertion holds because $f.a$ is the set of all the packets where each packet can be accepted in every reachable state of f and $g.a$ is the set of all the packets that can be accepted in the initial state of f.
Proof of ii: Note that g is a stateless firewall. By Theorem 4.4.1, this assertion holds.
Proof of iii: This assertion holds because $g.b$ is the set of all the packets that can be accepted in the initial state of f, and $f.a$ is the set of all the packets where each packet can be accepted in some reachable state of f. $\Box$

Recall that a firewall f is truly stateful iff $f.a \subset f.b$. By Theorem 4.4.2, one way to prove that a firewall f, whose stateless derivative is denoted g, is truly stateful is to prove that the following two conditions hold:

 i. $f.a = g.a$;
 ii. $g.b \subset f.b$

We call firewalls that satisfy the first condition *conforming firewalls*; and call firewalls that satisfy the second condition *proper firewalls*.

4.5   Firewall Properties

In this section, we discuss how to verify that a firewall is conforming or proper.

4.5.1   *Conforming Firewalls*

Before we give a theorem on how to verify that a firewall is conforming, we need to introduce the two concepts of complementary rules and accepting rules.

Let rule r, that appears in the stateless section of some firewall, be of the form

$$F_1 \in S_1 \land \cdots \land F_d \in S_d \land tag \in S_t \to \langle decision \rangle$$

Rule r is *complementary* iff the set S_t does not contain the value 0. Rule r is *accepting* iff the $\langle decision \rangle$ of r contains the command *"accept"*.

The following theorem can be used to verify that a firewall is conforming.

Theorem 4.5.1. A firewall f is conforming if every complementary rule in the stateless section of f is accepting.

Proof of Theorem 4.5.1: Given a firewall f and its stateless derivative g, we know $f.a \subseteq g.a$ according to Theorem 4.4.2. Next we prove that if every complementary rule of f is accepting, then $g.a \subseteq f.a$. For any packet $p \in g.a$, there is an accepting rule r whose predicate is of the form

$$F_1 \in S_1 \land \cdots \land F_d \in S_d \land tag \in S_t$$

such that $0 \in S_t$, and the packet p with tag value being 0 matches r but does not match any rule listed above r. Because every complementary rule is an accepting rule, every packet with a certain tag value that satisfies

$$F_1 \in S_1 \land \cdots \land F_d \in S_d \land tag \in (D(tag) - S_t)$$

is accepted by the firewall. Here $D(tag)$ denotes the domain of tag. So, no matter what the tag value of p is, p is accepted by f. Therefore, $p \in f.a.\square$

As an example, we use Theorem 4.5.1 to prove that the firewall in Figure 4.2 is conforming as follows. This firewall has only one complementary rule, which is rule $r_3 : I \in \{0\} \land P \in \{icmp\} \land T \in \{pong\} \land tag \in \{1\} \to accept$. And rule r_3 is an accepting rule. Therefore, this firewall is conforming.

4.5.2   *Proper Firewalls*

Based on our experience in designing firewalls, most firewalls are conforming. By Theorem 4.4.2, a conforming firewall is truly stateful iff it is proper. Next we discuss how to verify that a firewall is proper.

A firewall is proper iff its acceptable set is a proper superset of the acceptable set of its stateless derivative. For a firewall to be proper, we first need to make sure that its state does not remain empty forever. We call such firewalls grounded. More precisely, grounded firewalls are defined as follows.

Let f be a firewall whose stateless section consists of n rules $r_1, r_2, \cdots, r_n$:

$$r_1 : \quad P_1 \to \langle decision_1 \rangle$$

$$r_2 : \quad P_2 \rightarrow \langle decision_2 \rangle$$

$$\cdots$$

$$r_n : \quad P_n \rightarrow \langle decision_n \rangle$$

A rule r_k, where $1 \leq k \leq n$, is called a *ground rule* iff the following three conditions hold:

i. r_k is non-complementary;

ii. $\langle decision_k \rangle$ is "*accept*; *insert*" or "*accept*; *insert*; *remove*";

iii. $\sim P_1 \wedge \sim P_2 \wedge \cdots \wedge \sim P_{k-1} \wedge P_k$ is satisfiable by at least one packet.

A firewall is *grounded* iff it has a ground rule.

A ground rule of a grounded firewall guarantees that in the initial state of the firewall, there exists at least one packet that can be accepted and inserted into the state of the firewall.

To test whether a firewall is grounded, we can go through each rule and test whether it is a ground rule according to the above definition. Once we find a ground rule in a firewall, we know that the firewall is grounded. For example, consider the firewall in Figure 4.4. The second rule in the stateless section of this firewall is a ground rule because (1) it is non-complementary; (2) its decision is "*accept*; *insert*"; and (3) $\sim P_1 \wedge P_2$ is satisfiable. Note that $\sim P_1 \wedge P_2 = I \in \{1\} \wedge S \in [0, \alpha - 1] \cup [\alpha + 1, 2^{32}) \wedge D \in all \wedge DP \in all \wedge P \in all \wedge tag \in all$, where α denotes the integer formed by the four bytes of the IP address 192.1.2.3. Therefore, this firewall is grounded.

For a grounded firewall to be proper, we need to show that there exists at least one packet, denoted p, such that (1) p is discarded by the stateless derivative of the firewall, (2) p can be accepted by the firewall in some state. As an example, we show how to verify that a grounded firewall is proper by examining the firewall example in Figure 4.2 as follows. For this firewall, we assume that each packet consists of the fields of I, S, D, P, T, ID, and SN. Consider the two packets p' and p in the following table. It is straightforward to verify that packet p is discarded by the stateless derivative of this firewall (because of rule r_4). At any state of this firewall, p' is accepted and inserted into the state because of rule r_1. Because of the stateful rule R_1 and the stateless rule r_3, as long as p' is in the state, packet p is accepted. Therefore, this firewall is proper.

	I	S	D	P	T	ID	SN
p'	1	192.1.2.4	192.32.1.2	*icmp*	*ping*	10	200
p	0	192.32.1.2	192.1.2.4	*icmp*	*pong*	10	200

Chapter 5

Firewall Queries

Although a firewall is specified by a mere sequence of rules, understanding its function is by no means an easy task. Even understanding the implication of a single rule is difficult because one has to go through all the rules listed above that rule to figure out their logical relations. Understanding the function of an entire firewall is even more difficult because the firewall may have a large number of rules and the rules often conflict with each other. Furthermore, firewall administrators often have to analyze legacy firewalls that were written by different administrators, at different times, and for different reasons. Effective methods and tools for analyzing firewalls, therefore, are crucial to the success of firewalls.

An effective way to assist humans in understanding and analyzing firewalls is by issuing firewall queries. Firewall queries are questions concerning the function of a firewall. Examples of firewall queries are "Which computers in the outside Internet cannot send email to the mail server in a private network?" and "Which computers in the private network can receive BOOTP[1] packets from the outside Internet?".

Figuring out answers to these firewall queries is of tremendous help for a firewall administrator to understand and analyze the function of the firewall. For example, assuming the specification of a firewall requires that all computers in the outside Internet, except a known malicious host, are able to send email to the mail server in the private network, a firewall administrator can test whether the firewall satisfies this requirement by issuing a firewall query "Which computers in the outside Internet cannot send email to the mail server in the private network?". If the answer to this query con-

---

[1]The Bootp protocol is used by workstations and other devices to obtain IP addresses and other information about the network configuration of a private network. Since there is no need to offer the service outside a private network, and it may offer useful information to hackers, usually Bootp packets are blocked from entering a private network.

tains exactly the known malicious host, then the firewall administrator is assured that the firewall does satisfy this requirement. Otherwise the firewall administrator knows that the firewall fails to satisfy this requirement, and she needs to reconfigure the firewall. As another example, suppose that the specification of a firewall requires that any BOOTP packet from the outside Internet is to be blocked from entering the private network. To test whether the firewall satisfies this requirement, a firewall administrator can issue a firewall query "Which computers in the private network can receive BOOTP packets from the outside Internet?". If the answer to this query is an empty set, then the firewall administrator is assured that the firewall does satisfy this requirement. Otherwise the firewall administrator knows that the firewall fails to satisfy this requirement, and she needs to reconfigure the firewall.

Firewall queries are also useful in a variety of other scenarios, such as firewall maintenance and firewall debugging. For a firewall administrator, checking whether a firewall satisfies certain conditions is part of daily maintenance activity. For example, if the administrator detects that a computer in the private network is under attack, the firewall administrator can issue queries to check which other computers in the private network are also vulnerable to the same type of attacks. In the process of designing a firewall, the designer can issue some firewall queries to detect design errors by checking whether the answers to the queries are consistent with the firewall specification.

To make firewall queries practically useful, two problems need to be solved: how to describe a firewall query and how to process a firewall query. The second problem is technically difficult. Recall that the rules in a firewall are sensitive to the rule order and the rules often conflict. The naive solution is to enumerate every packet specified by a query and check the decision for each packet. Clearly, this solution is infeasible. For example, to process the query "Which computers in the outside Internet cannot send any packet to the private network?", this naive solution needs to enumerate 2^{88} possible packet and check the decision of the firewall for each packet, which is infeasible.

There is little work that has been done on firewall queries. In [Mayer *et al.* (2000); Wool (2001)], a firewall analysis system that uses some specific firewall queries was presented. In [Mayer *et al.* (2000); Wool (2001)], a firewall query is described by a triple (a set of source addresses, a set of destination addresses, a set of services), where each service is a tuple (protocol type, destination port number). The semantics of such a query are "which

IP addresses in the set of source addresses can send which services in the set of services to which IP addresses in the set of destination addresses?".
We go beyond [Mayer *et al.* (2000); Wool (2001)] in the following two major aspects.

i. No algorithm for processing a firewall query over a sequence of rules was presented in [Mayer *et al.* (2000)] or [Wool (2001)]. Consequently, how fast and scalable that a firewall query can be processed remains unknown, while the efficiency of a firewall query processing algorithm is crucial in order to interact with a human user. In contrast, we present an efficient algorithm for processing a firewall query over a sequence of rules. Our firewall query algorithm takes less than 10 milliseconds to process a query over a firewall that has up to 10,000 rules.

ii. The query language described in [Mayer *et al.* (2000)] and [Wool (2001)] is too specific: it is only applicable to IP packets and it only concerns the four fields of source address, destination address, protocol type and destination port number. This makes the expressive power of the query language in [Mayer *et al.* (2000); Wool (2001)] limited. For example, even only considering IP packets, it cannot express a firewall query concerning source port numbers or application fields. In contrast, our Structured Firewall Query Language is capable of expressing firewall queries with arbitrary fields.

In [Hazelhurst *et al.* (2000)], some ad-hoc "what if" questions that are similar to firewall queries were discussed. However, no algorithm was presented for processing the proposed "what if" questions. In [Eronen and Zitting (2001)], expert systems were proposed to analyze firewall rules. Clearly, building an expert system just for analyzing a firewall is overwrought and impractical.

In this chapter, we present solutions to both problems. First, we introduce a simple and effective SQL-like query language, called the Structured Firewall Query Language (SFQL), for describing firewall queries. This language uses queries of the form *"select...from...where..."*. Second, we present a theorem, called the Firewall Query Theorem, as the foundation for developing firewall query processing algorithms. Third, we present an efficient query processing algorithm that uses Firewall Decision Trees (FDTs) as its core data structure. For a given firewall of a sequence of rules, we first construct an equivalent FDT using the construction algorithm introduced in Chapter 2.8. Then the FDT is used as the core data structure of this query processing algorithm for answering each firewall query. Experimental results show that our firewall query processing algorithm is very efficient: it takes less than 10 milliseconds to process a query over a firewall that has up to 10,000 rules. Clearly, our firewall query processing algorithm is fast enough in interacting with firewall administrators.

Note that firewalls that we consider in this chapter are stateless firewalls. Also note that the queries of a firewall are intended primarily for the administrator of the firewall to use. For a firewall that protects a private network, neither normal users in the private network nor the outsiders of the private network are able to query the firewall.

5.1   Structured Firewall Query Language

5.1.1   *Firewalls*

In this section, we present the actual syntax of the firewall query language and show how to use this language to describe firewall queries.

We use Σ to denote the set of all packets. It follows that Σ is a finite set and $|\Sigma| = |D(F_1)| \times \cdots \times |D(F_n)|$. Given a firewall f, each packet p in Σ is mapped by f to a decision, denoted $f(p)$, in the set $\{accept, discard\}$. Two firewalls f and f' are equivalent, denoted $f \equiv f'$, iff for any packet p in Σ, the condition $f(p) = f'(p)$ holds. This equivalence relation is symmetric, self-reflective, and transitive.

A firewall consists of a sequence of rules. Each rule is of the following format:

$$(F_1 \in S_1) \wedge \cdots \wedge (F_d \in S_d) \rightarrow \langle decision \rangle$$

where each S_i is a nonempty subset of $D(F_i)$, and the $\langle decision \rangle$ is either *accept* or *discard*. If $S_i = D(F_i)$, we can replace $(F_i \in S_i)$ by $(F_i \in all)$, or remove the conjunct $(F_i \in D(F_i))$ altogether. Some existing firewall products, such as Linux's ipchain, require that S_i be represented in a prefix format such as 192.168.0.0/16, where 16 means that the prefix is the first 16 bits of 192.168.0.0 in a binary format. In this chapter, we choose to represent S_i as a nonempty set of nonnegative integers because of two reasons. First, any set of nonnegative integers can be automatically converted to a set of prefixes (see [Gupta and McKeown (2001)]). Second, set representations are more convenient in mathematical manipulations.

A packet $(p_1, \cdots, p_d)$ *matches* a rule $(F_1 \in S_1) \wedge \cdots \wedge (F_d \in S_d) \rightarrow \langle decision \rangle$ iff the condition $(p_1 \in S_1) \wedge \cdots \wedge (p_d \in S_d)$ holds. Since a packet may match more than one rule in a firewall, each packet is mapped to the decision of the first rule that the packet matches. The predicate of the last rule in a firewall is usually a tautology to ensure that every packet has at least one matching rule in the firewall.

Here we give an example of a simple firewall. In this example, we assume that each packet only has two fields: S (source address) and D (destination address), and both fields have the same domain $[1, 10]$. This firewall consists of the sequence of rules in Figure 5.1. Let f_1 be the name of this firewall.

$$r_1 : \; S \in [4, 7] \;\; \wedge \;\; D \in [6, 8] \; \rightarrow \; accept$$
$$r_2 : \; S \in [3, 8] \;\; \wedge \;\; D \in [2, 9] \; \rightarrow \; discard$$
$$r_3 : \; S \in [1, 10] \; \wedge \;\; D \in [1, 10] \rightarrow \; accept$$

Fig. 5.1 Firewall f_1

5.1.2 *Query Language*

A *query*, denoted Q, in our Structured Firewall Query Language (SFQL) is of the following format:

$$
\begin{aligned}
&\textbf{select } F_i \\
&\textbf{from } \; f \\
&\textbf{where} \, (F_1 \in S_1) \wedge \cdots \wedge (F_d \in S_d) \wedge (\textbf{decision} = \langle dec \rangle)
\end{aligned}
$$

where F_i is one of the fields $F_1, \cdots, F_d$, f is a firewall, each S_j is a nonempty subset of the domain $D(F_j)$ of field F_j, and $\langle dec \rangle$ is either *accept* or *discard*.

The result of query Q, denoted $Q.result$, is the following set:

$$\{p_i | (p_1, \cdots, p_d) \text{ is a packet in } \Sigma, \text{ and}$$
$$(p_1 \in S_1) \wedge \cdots \wedge (p_d \in S_d) \wedge (f((p_1, \cdots, p_d)) = \langle dec \rangle)\}$$

Recall that Σ denotes the set of all packets, and $f((p_1, \cdots, p_d))$ denotes the decision to which firewall f maps the packet $(p_1, \cdots, p_d)$.

We can get the above set by first finding all the packets $(p_1, \cdots, p_d)$ in Σ such that the following condition

$$(p_1 \in S_1) \wedge \cdots \wedge (p_d \in S_d) \wedge (f((p_1, \cdots, p_d)) = \langle dec \rangle)$$

holds, then projecting all these packets to the field F_i.

For example, a question to the firewall in Figure 5.1, "Which computers whose addresses are in the set $[4, 8]$ can send packets to the machine whose address is 6?", can be formulated as the following query using SFQL:

>   **select** S
>   **from** f_1
>   **where** $(S \in \{[4, 8]\}) \wedge (D \in \{6\}) \wedge (\textbf{decision} = accept)$

The result of this query is $\{4, 5, 6, 7\}$.

As another example, a question to the firewall in Figure 5.1, "Which computer cannot send packets to the computer whose address is 6?", can be formulated as the following query using SFQL:

>   **select** S
>   **from** f_1
>   **where** $(S \in all) \wedge (D \in \{6\}) \wedge (\textbf{decision} = discard)$

The result of this query is $\{3, 8\}$.

Next we give more examples on how to use SFQL to describe firewall queries.

5.2   Firewall Query Examples

In this section, we describe some example firewall queries using SFQL. Let f be the name of the firewall that resides on the gateway router in Figure 5.2. This gateway router has two interfaces: interface 0, which connects the gateway router to the outside Internet, and interface 1, which connects the gateway router to the inside local network. In these examples, we assume each packet has the following five fields: I (Interface), S (Source IP), D (Destination IP), N (Destination Port), P (Protocol Type).

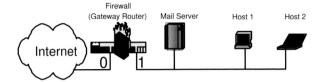

Fig. 5.2   Firewall f

Question 1:
   Which computers in the private network protected by the firewall f can receive BOOTP[2] packets from the outside Internet?
Query Q_1:
   select D
   from f
   where $(I \in \{0\}) \wedge (S \in all) \wedge (D \in all) \wedge (N \in \{67, 68\})$
          $\wedge (P \in \{udp\}) \wedge (\textbf{decision} = accept)$
Answer to question 1 is $Q_1.result$.

Question 2:
   Which ports on the mail server protected by the firewall f are open?
Query Q_2:
   select N
   from f
   where $(I \in \{0, 1\}) \wedge (S \in all) \wedge (D \in \{Mail\ Server\}) \wedge (N \in all)$
          $\wedge (P \in all) \wedge (\textbf{decision} = accept)$
Answer to question 2 is $Q_2.result$.

---

[2]Bootp packets are UDP packets and use port number 67 or 68.

Question 3:
   Which computers in the outside Internet cannot send SMTP[3] packets
   to the mail server protected by the firewall f?
Query Q_3:
   select S
   from f
   where $(I \in \{0\}) \land (S \in all) \land (D \in \{Mail\ Server\}) \land (N \in \{25\})$
       $\land (P \in \{tcp\}) \land (\textbf{decision} = discard)$
Answer to question 3 is $Q_3.result$.

Question 4:
   Which computers in the outside Internet cannot send any packet to
   the private network protected by the firewall f?
Query Q_4:
   select S
   from f
   where $(I \in \{0\}) \land (S \in all) \land (D \in all) \land (N \in all) \land (P \in all)$
       $\land (\textbf{decision} = accept)$
Answer to question 4 is $T - Q_4.result$, where T is the set of
all IP addresses outside of the private network

Question 5:
   Which computers in the outside Internet can send SMTP packets to
   host 1 and host 2 in the private network protected by the firewall f?
Query Q_{5a}:
   select S
   from f
   where $(I \in \{0\}) \land (S \in all) \land (D \in \{Host\ 1\}) \land (N \in \{25\})$
       $\land (P \in \{tcp\}) \land (\textbf{decision} = accept)$
Query Q_{5b}:
   select S
   from f
   where $(I \in \{0\}) \land (S \in all) \land (D \in \{Host\ 2\}) \land (N \in \{25\})$
       $\land (P \in \{tcp\}) \land (\textbf{decision} = accept)$
Answer to question 5 is $Q_{5a}.result \cap Q_{5b}.result$.

---

[3]SMTP stands for Simple Mail Transfer Protocol. SMTP packets are TCP packets and
use port number 25.

5.3 Firewall Query Processing

In this section, we discuss how to process a firewall query for consistent firewalls. Consistent firewalls and inconsistent firewalls are defined as follows:

Definition 5.3.1 (Consistent Firewalls). A firewall is called a consistent firewall iff any two rules in the firewall do not conflict.

Definition 5.3.2 (Inconsistent Firewalls). A firewall is called an inconsistent firewall iff there are at least two rules in the firewall that conflict.

Recall that two rules in a firewall conflict iff they have different decisions and there is at least one packet that can match both rules. For example, the first two rules in the firewall in Figure 5.1, namely r_1 and r_2, conflict. Note that for any two rules in a consistent firewall, if they overlap, i.e., there is at least one packet can match both rules, they have the same decision. So, given a packet and a consistent firewall, all the rules in the firewall that the packet matches have the same decision. Figure 5.1 shows an example of an inconsistent firewall, and Figure 5.3 shows an example of a consistent firewall. In these two firewall examples, we assume that each packet only has two fields: S (source address) and D (destination address), and both fields have the same domain $[1, 10]$.

$$
\begin{aligned}
r_1' &: S \in [4,7] & \wedge\ D \in [6,8] & \to a \\
r_2' &: S \in [4,7] & \wedge\ D \in [2,5] \cup [9,9] & \to d \\
r_3' &: S \in [4,7] & \wedge\ D \in [1,1] \cup [10,10] & \to a \\
r_4' &: S \in [3,3] \cup [8,8] & \wedge\ D \in [2,9] & \to d \\
r_5' &: S \in [3,3] \cup [8,8] & \wedge\ D \in [1,1] \cup [10,10] & \to a \\
r_6' &: S \in [1,2] \cup [9,10] & \wedge\ D \in [1,10] & \to a
\end{aligned}
$$

Fig. 5.3   Consistent firewall f_2

Our interest in consistent firewalls is twofold. First, each inconsistent firewall can be converted to an equivalent consistent firewall, as described in Section 5.4. Second, as shown in the following theorem, it is easier to process queries for consistent firewalls than for inconsistent firewalls.

Theorem 5.3.1 (Firewall Query Theorem). Let Q be a query of the following form:

select F_i
from f
where $(F_1 \in S_1) \wedge \cdots \wedge (F_d \in S_d) \wedge (\textbf{decision} = \langle dec \rangle)$

If f is a consistent firewall that consists of n rules $r_1, \cdots, r_n$, then we have

$$Q.result = \bigcup_{j=1}^{n} Q.r_j$$

where each rule r_j is of the form

$$(F_1 \in S_1') \wedge \cdots \wedge (F_d \in S_d') \to \langle dec' \rangle$$

and the quantity of $Q.r_j$ is defined as follows:

$$Q.r_j = \begin{cases} S_i \cap S_i' & \text{if } (S_1 \cap S_1' \neq \emptyset) \wedge \cdots \wedge (S_d \cap S_d' \neq \emptyset) \wedge (\langle dec \rangle = \langle dec' \rangle), \\ \emptyset & \text{otherwise} \end{cases}$$

$\square$

The Firewall Query Theorem implies a simple query processing algorithm: given a consistent firewall f that consists of n rules $r_1, \cdots, r_n$ and a query Q, compute $Q.r_j$ for each j, then $\bigcup_{j=1}^{n} Q.r_j$ is the result of query Q. We call this algorithm the *rule-based firewall query processing algorithm*. Figure 5.4 shows the pseudocode of this algorithm.

Rule − based Firewall Query Processing Algorithm
Input : (1) A consistent firewall f that consists of n rules: $r_1, \cdots, r_n$,
              (2) A query Q:
                  select F_i
                  from f
                  where $(F_1 \in S_1) \wedge \cdots \wedge (F_d \in S_d) \wedge (\textbf{decision} = \langle dec \rangle)$
Output: Result of query Q
Steps:
1. $Q.result := \emptyset$;
2. **for** $j := 1$ **to** n **do** /*Let $r_j = (F_1 \in S_1') \wedge \cdots \wedge (F_d \in S_d') \to \langle dec' \rangle$*/
     if $(S_1 \cap S_1' \neq \emptyset) \wedge \cdots \wedge (S_d \cap S_d' \neq \emptyset) \wedge (\langle dec \rangle = \langle dec' \rangle)$
     then $Q.result := Q.result \cup (S_i \cap S_i')$;
3. **return** $Q.result$;

Fig. 5.4   Rule-based Firewall Query Processing Algorithm

5.4   FDT-based Firewall Query Processing Algorithm

Observe that multiple rules in a consistent firewall may share the same prefix. For example, in the consistent firewall in Figure 5.3, the first three rules, namely r'_1, r'_2, r'_3, share the same prefix $S \in [4, 7]$. Thus, if we apply the above query processing algorithm in Figure 5.4 to answer a query, for instance, whose "where clause" contains the conjunct $S \in \{3\}$, over the firewall in Figure 5.3, then the algorithm will repeat three times the calculation of $\{3\} \cap [4, 7]$. Clearly, repeated calculations are not desirable for efficiency purposes.

In this section, we present a firewall query processing method that has no repeated calculations and can be applied to both consistent and inconsistent firewalls. This method consists of two steps. First, convert the firewall (whether consistent or inconsistent) to an equivalent firewall decision tree. Second, use this FDT as the core data structure for processing queries. We call the algorithm that uses an FDT to process queries the *FDT-based firewall query processing algorithm*. Firewall Decision Trees are defined as follows.

Definition 5.4.1 (Firewall Decision Tree). A Firewall Decision Tree t over fields $F_1, \cdots, F_d$ is a special firewall decision diagram that has the following two additional properties:

i. Each node has at most one incoming edge (i.e., t is a directed tree).
ii. Each decision path contains d nonterminal nodes, and the i-th node from the root is labelled F_i for every i where $1 \le i \le d$.

Figure 5.5 shows an example of an FDT named t_3. In this example, we assume that each packet only has two fields: S (source address) and D (destination address), and both fields have the same domain $[1, 10]$.

Considering the FDT t_3 in Figure 5.5, Figure 5.3 shows all the six rules in $t_3.rules$.

Given a sequence of rules, an equivalent FDT can be constructed using the construction algorithm described in Chapter 2.8.

The pseudocode of the FDT-based firewall query processing algorithm is shown in Figure 5.6. Here we use $e.t$ to denote the (target) node that the edge e points to, and we use $t.root$ to denote the root of FDT t.

The above FDT-based firewall query processing algorithm has two inputs, an FDT t and an SFQL query Q. The algorithm starts by traversing the FDT from its root. Let F_j be the label of the root. For each

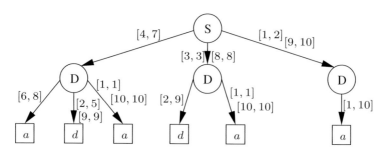

Fig. 5.5　Firewall Decision Tree t_3

outgoing edge e of the root, we compute $I(e) \cap S_j$. If $I(e) \cap S_j = \emptyset$, we skip edge e and do not traverse the subgraph that e points to. If $I(e) \cap S_j \neq \emptyset$, then we continue to traverse the subgraph that e points to in a similar fashion. Whenever a terminal node is encountered, we compare the label of the terminal node and $\langle dec \rangle$. If they are the same, assuming the rule defined by the decision path containing the terminal node is $(F_1 \in S_1') \wedge \cdots \wedge (F_d \in S_d') \rightarrow \langle dec' \rangle$, then we add $S_i \cap S_i'$ to $Q.result$.

5.5　Experimental Results

So far we have presented two firewall query processing algorithms, the rule-based algorithm in Section 5.3 and the FDT-based algorithm in Section 5.4. In this section, we evaluate the efficiency of both algorithms. In the absence of publicly available firewalls, we create synthetic firewalls according to the characteristics of real-life packet classifiers discussed in [Baboescu *et al.* (2003); Gupta (2000)]. Note that a firewall is also a packet classifier. Each rule has the following five fields: interface, source IP address, destination IP address, destination port number and protocol type. The programs are implemented in SUN Java JDK 1.4. The experiments were carried out on a SunBlade 2000 machine running Solaris 9 with 1Ghz CPU and 1 GB of memory.

　　Figure 5.7 shows the average execution time of both algorithms versus the total number of rules in the original (maybe inconsistent) firewalls. The horizontal axis indicates the total number of rules in the original firewalls, and the vertical axis indicates the average execution time (in milliseconds) for processing a firewall query. Note that in Figure 5.7, the execution time of the FDT-based firewall query processing algorithm does not include

FDT – based Firewall Query Processing Algorithm
Input : (1)An FDT t,
       (2)A query Q: **select** F_i
                     from t
                     where $(F_1 \in S_1) \wedge \cdots \wedge (F_d \in S_d)$
                              $\wedge (\textbf{decision} = \langle dec \rangle)$
Output : Result of query Q
Steps:
1. $Q.result := \emptyset$;
2. **CHECK**($t.root$, $(F_1 \in S_1) \wedge \cdots \wedge (F_d \in S_d) \wedge (\textbf{decision} = \langle dec \rangle$)
3. **return** $Q.result$;

CHECK(v, $(F_1 \in S_1) \wedge \cdots \wedge (F_d \in S_d) \wedge (\textbf{decision} = \langle dec \rangle)$)
1. **if** (v is a terminal node) and ($F(v) = \langle dec \rangle$) **then**
   (1) Let $(F_1 \in S_1') \wedge \cdots \wedge (F_d \in S_d') \rightarrow \langle dec' \rangle$ be the rule
       defined by the decision path containing node v;
   (2) $Q.result := Q.result \cup (S_i \cap S_i')$;
2. **if** (v is a nonterminal node) **then** /*Let F_j be the label of v*/
     for each edge e in $E(v)$ **do**
        if $I(e) \cap S_j \neq \emptyset$ **then**
           CHECK($e.t$, $(F_1 \in S_1) \wedge \cdots \wedge (F_d \in S_d) \wedge (\textbf{decision} = \langle dec \rangle)$)

Fig. 5.6   FDT-based Firewall Query Processing Algorithm

the FDT construction time because the conversion from a firewall to an equivalent FDT is performed only once for each firewall, not for each query. Similarly, the execution time of the rule-based firewall query processing algorithm does not include the time for converting an inconsistent firewall to an equivalent consistent firewall because this conversion is performed only once for each firewall, not for each query.

From Figure 5.7, we can see that the FDT-based firewall query processing algorithm is much more efficient than the rule-based firewall query processing algorithm. For example, for processing a query over an inconsistent firewall that has 10,000 rules, the FDT-based query processing algorithm uses about 10 milliseconds, while the rule-based query processing algorithm uses about 100 milliseconds. The experimental results in Figure

5.7 confirm our analysis that the FDT-based query processing algorithm saves execution time by reducing repeated calculations.

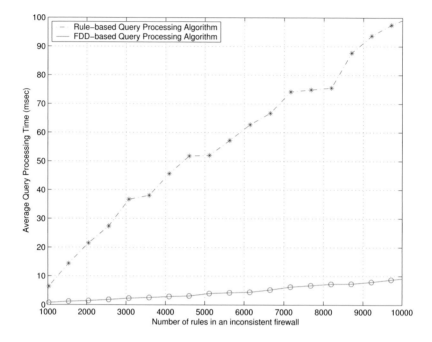

Fig. 5.7   Query Processing Time vs. Number of rules

Chapter 6

Firewall Redundancy Detection

Firewalls often have redundant rules. A rule in a firewall is redundant iff removing the rule does not change the function of the firewall, i.e., does not change the decision of the firewall for every packet. For example, consider the firewall in Figure 6.1, whose geometric representation is in Figure 6.2. This firewall consists of four rules r_1 through r_4. The domain of field F_1 is $[1, 100]$.

$$r_1 : F_1 \in [1, \ 50] \ \rightarrow accept$$
$$r_2 : F_1 \in [40, \ 90] \ \rightarrow discard$$
$$r_3 : F_1 \in [30, \ 60] \ \rightarrow accept$$
$$r_4 : F_1 \in [51, \ 100] \rightarrow discard$$

Fig. 6.1   A simple firewall

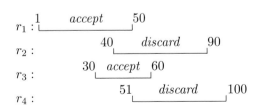

Fig. 6.2   Geometric representation of Figure 6.1

We have the following two observations concerning the redundant rules in the firewall in Figure 6.1.

i. Rule r_3 is redundant. This is because the first matching rule for all packets where $F_1 \in [30, 50]$ is r_1, and the first matching rule for all packets where $F_1 \in [51, 60]$ is r_2. Therefore, there are no packets whose first matching rule is r_3. We call r_3 an upward redundant rule. A rule r in a firewall is *upward redundant* iff there are no packets whose first matching rule is r. Geometrically, a rule is upward redundant in a firewall iff the rule is overlayed by some rules listed above it.

ii. Rule r_2 becomes redundant after r_3 is removed. Note that r_2 is the first matching rule for all packets where $F_1 \in [51, 90]$. However, if both r_2 and r_3 are removed, the first matching rule for all those packets becomes r_4 instead of r_2. This is acceptable since both r_2 and r_4 have the same decision. We call r_2 a downward redundant rule. A rule r in a firewall, where no rule is upward redundant, is *downward redundant* iff for each packet, whose first matching rule is r, the first matching rule below r has the same decision as r.

Redundant rules are harmful in terms of the performance a firewall. When a firewall receives an incoming or outgoing packet, the firewall needs to find the first rule that the packet matches. This processing time is critical because it affects the delay of every packet. In general, the smaller the number of rules that a firewall has, the faster the firewall can map a packet to the decision of the first rule the packet matches. The algorithm that maps a packet to the decision of the first rule that the packet matches uses either $O(n)$ space and $O((\log n)^{d-1})$ time or $O(n^d)$ space and $O(\log n)$ time, where n is the total number of rules and d is the total number of distinct packet fields that are examined [Gupta (2000)]. Reducing the number of rules is especially useful for the firewalls that use TCAM (Ternary Content Addressable Memory). Such firewalls use $O(n)$ space (where n is the number of rules) and constant time in mapping a packet to a decision. Despite the high performance of such TCAM-based firewalls, TCAM has very limited size and consumes much more power as the number of rules increases. Size limitation and power consumption are the two major issues for TCAM-based firewalls.

Redundant rules are harmful in terms of the correctness a firewall. First, if a firewall has many redundant rules, it may indicate that the firewall rules are not well designed. A badly designed firewall may have many errors. An error in firewall rules means that some illegitimate packets are identified as being legitimate, or some legitimate packets are identified as being illegitimate. This will either allow unauthorized access from the outside Internet to the private network, or disable some legitimate communication between the private network and the outside Internet. In fact, it has been observed that most firewall security breaches are caused by errors in firewall rules [Wool (2004)].

Redundant rules are harmful in terms of the understandability a firewall. A redundant rule could be misleading and give a false sense of security. For example, suppose a firewall has a redundant rule "discard all Slammer worm packets", this rule could give the administrator the impression that all the Slammer worm packets are indeed discarded, which in fact may not be true since this rule is redundant.

Previous work on redundant rules includes [Gupta (2000); Al-Shaer and Hamed (2003a,b, 2004)]. In [Gupta (2000)], two special types of redundant rules are identified: backward redundant rules and forward redundant rules. A rule r in a firewall is backward redundant iff there exists another rule r' listed above r such that all packets that match r also match r'. Clearly, a backward redundant rule is an upward redundant rule, but not vice versa. For example, rule r_3 in Figure 6.1 is upward redundant, but not backward redundant. A rule r in a firewall is forward redundant iff there exists another rule r' listed below r such that the following three conditions hold: (1) all packets that match r also match r', (2) r and r' have the same decision, (3) for each rule r'' listed between r and r', either r and r'' have the same decision, or no packet matches both r and r''. Clearly, a forward redundant rule is a downward redundant rule, but not vice versa. For example, rule r_2 in Figure 6.1, assuming r_3 has been removed previously, is downward redundant, but not forward redundant. It has been observed in [Gupta (2000)] that 15% of the rules in real-life firewalls are backward redundant or forward redundant.

The redundant rules identified in [Al-Shaer and Hamed (2003a,b, 2004)] are similar to those identified in [Gupta (2000)], except that for the case of backward redundant rules, they require that the two rules r and r' must have the same decision, which is in fact unnecessary.

The bottom line is that the set of redundant rules identified by previous work is incomplete. In other words, given a firewall, after we remove the redundant rules identified in previous work, the firewall still possibly has redundant rules. So, how to detect all the redundant rules in a firewall? This is a hard problem and this problem has never been addressed previously.

In this chapter, we solve the problem of detecting all redundant rules in a firewall. First, we give a necessary and sufficient condition for identifying all redundant rules. Based on this condition, we categorize redundant rules into upward redundant rules and downward redundant rules. Second, we present two efficient graph based algorithms for detecting these two types of redundant rules. The experimental results show that these two algorithms are very efficient.

There are two ways to apply the procedure redundancy detection and removal. One way is to apply it prominently with user's attention for detecting firewall errors. For every redundant rule detected, the firewall administrator can examine whether the rule should be removed; if not, then clearly the firewall has errors and the administrator can further investigate how to correct them. The other way is to apply the firewall redundancy detection and removal procedure transparently without user's attention for improving firewall performance. In other words, the interface of a firewall to the firewall administrator is always the original sequence of rules with redundant rules, while what is actually used in the firewall is the compact sequence of rules without redundant rules. Whenever the original sequence of rules is updated, the firewall redundancy detection and removal procedure is automatically applied, and the resulting compact sequence of rules is henceforth used in the firewall.

The rest of this chapter is organized as follows. We give a necessary and sufficient condition for identifying upward and downward redundant rules in Section 6.1. The upward and downward redundancy removal algorithms are presented in Section 6.2 and 6.3. The experimental results are shown in Section 6.4.

6.1   Firewall Redundant Rules

A sequence of rules $\langle r_1, \cdots, r_n \rangle$ is *comprehensive* iff for any packet p in Σ, there is at least one rule in $\langle r_1, \cdots, r_n \rangle$ that p matches. A sequence of rules needs to be comprehensive for it to serve as a firewall. From now on, we assume that each firewall is comprehensive. Henceforth, the predicate of the last rule in a firewall can always be replaced by $(F_1 \in D(F_1)) \wedge \cdots \wedge (F_d \in D(F_d))$ without changing the function of the firewall. In the rest of this chapter, we assume that the predicate of the last rule in a firewall is $(F_1 \in D(F_1)) \wedge \cdots \wedge (F_d \in D(F_d))$. It follows from this assumption that any postfix of a firewall is comprehensive, i.e., given a firewall $\langle r_1, r_2, \cdots, r_n \rangle$, we know that $\langle r_i, r_{i+1}, \cdots, r_n \rangle$ is comprehensive for each i, $1 \leq i \leq n$. This assumption is crucial for our downward redundancy removal algorithm in Section 6.3.

We use $f(p)$ to denote the decision to which a firewall f maps a packet *p*. Two firewalls f and f' are equivalent, denoted $f \equiv f'$, iff for any packet p in Σ, $f(p) = f'(p)$ holds. This equivalence relation is symmetric, self-reflective, and transitive. Using the concept of equivalent firewalls, we define redundant rules as follows.

Definition 6.1.1. *A rule r is redundant in a firewall f iff the resulting firewall f' after removing rule r is equivalent to f.*

Before introducing our redundancy theorem, we define two important concepts that are associated with each rule in a firewall: matching set and resolving set. Consider a firewall f that consists of n rules $\langle r_1, r_2, \cdots, r_n \rangle$. The *matching set* of a rule r_i in this firewall is the set of all packets that match r_i. The *resolving set* of a rule r_i in this firewall is the set of all packets that match r_i, but do not match any r_j where $j < i$. For example, consider rule r_2 in Figure 6.1: its matching set is the set of all the packets whose F_1 field is in $[40, 90]$; and its resolving set is the set of all the packets whose F_1 field is in $[51, 90]$. The matching set of a rule r_i is denoted $M(r_i)$, and the resolving set of a rule r_i is denoted $R(r_i, f)$. Note that the matching set of a rule depends only on the rule itself, while the resolving set of a rule depends both on the rule and on all the rules listed above it in a firewall.

The following theorem, whose proof is in the Appendix, states several important properties of matching sets and resolving sets.

Theorem 6.1.1 (Resolving Set Theorem). Let f be any firewall that consists of n rules: $\langle r_1, r_2, \cdots, r_n \rangle$. The following four conditions hold:

i. Equality: $\bigcup_{j=1}^{i} M(r_j) = \bigcup_{j=1}^{i} R(r_j, f)$ for each i, $1 \leq i \leq n$
ii. Dependency: $R(r_i, f) = M(r_i) - \bigcup_{j=1}^{i-1} R(r_j, f)$ for each i, $1 \leq i \leq n$
iii. Determinism: $R(r_i, f) \cap R(r_j, f) = \emptyset$ for each $i \neq j$
iv. Comprehensiveness: $\bigcup_{i=1}^{n} R(r_i, f) = \Sigma$ $\qquad\qquad$ □

The redundancy theorem below gives a necessary and sufficient condition for identifying redundant rules. Note that we use the notation $\langle r_{i+1}, r_{i+2}, \cdots, r_n \rangle(p)$ to denote the decision to which the firewall $\langle r_{i+1}, r_{i+2}, \cdots, r_n \rangle$ maps packet p.

Theorem 6.1.2 (Redundancy Theorem). Let f be any firewall that consists of n rules: $\langle r_1, r_2, \cdots, r_n \rangle$. A rule r_i is *redundant* in f iff one of the following two conditions holds:

i. $R(r_i, f) = \emptyset$,

ii. $R(r_i, f) \neq \emptyset$, and for any p that $p \in R(r_i, f)$, $\langle r_{i+1}, r_{i+2}, \cdots, r_n \rangle(p)$
yields the same decision as that of r_i.   □

The correctness of this theorem is quite straightforward to argue. Note
that removing rule r_i from firewall f only possibly affects the decision
of the packets in $R(r_i, f)$. If $R(r_i, f) = \emptyset$, then r_i is clearly redundant.
If $R(r_i, f) \neq \emptyset$, and for any p that $p \in R(r_i, f)$, $\langle r_{i+1}, r_{i+2}, \cdots, r_n \rangle(p)$
yields the same as that of r_i, then r_i is redundant because removing r_i
does not affect the decision of the packets in $R(r_i, f)$. The redundancy
theorem allows us to categorize redundant rules into upward and downward
redundant rules.

Definition 6.1.2. *A rule that satisfies condition 1 in the redundancy theorem is called upward redundant. A rule that satisfies condition 2 in the
redundancy theorem is called downward redundant.*

Consider the example firewall f in Figure 6.1. Rule r_3 is an upward
redundant rule because $R(r_3, f) = \emptyset$. Let f' be the resulting firewall by
removing rule r_3 from f. Then rule r_2 is downward redundant in f'.

6.2   Removing Upward Redundancy

In this section, we discuss how to remove upward redundant rules. By definition, a rule is upward redundant iff its resolving set is empty. Therefore,
in order to remove all upward redundant rules from a firewall, we need to
calculate resolving set for each rule in the firewall. How to represent a resolving set? In this chapter, we represent the resolving set of a rule by an
effective rule set of the rule. An effective rule set of a rule r in a firewall
f is a set of rules where the union of all the matching sets of these rules is
exactly the resolving set of rule r in f. More precisely, an effective rule set
of a rule r is defined as follows:

Definition 6.2.1. *Let r be a rule in a firewall f. A set of rules
$\{r_1', r_2', \cdots, r_k'\}$ is an effective rule set of r iff the following three conditions hold:*

i. $R(r, f) = \bigcup_{i=1}^{k} M(r_i')$,
ii. r_i' and r have the same decision for $1 \leq i \leq k$.   □

For example, consider the firewall in Figure 6.1. Then, $\{F_1 \in [1, 50] \rightarrow$
accept$\}$ is an effective rule set of rule r_1, $\{F_1 \in [51, 90] \rightarrow discard\}$ is

an effective rule set of rule r_2, $\emptyset$ is an effective rule set of rule r_3, and $\{F_1 \in [91, 100] \rightarrow discard\}$ is an effective rule set of rule r_4. Clearly, once we obtain an effective rule set of a rule r in a firewall f, we know the resolving set of the rule r in f, and consequently know whether the rule r is upward redundant in f. Note that by the definition of an effective rule set, if one effective rule set of a rule r is empty, then any effective rule set of the rule r is empty. Based on the above discussion, we have the following upward redundancy theorem:

Theorem 6.2.1 (Upward Redundancy Theorem). A rule r is upward redundant in a firewall iff an effective rule set of r is empty. $\qquad\square$

Based on the above upward redundancy theorem, the basic idea of our upward redundancy removal algorithm is as follows: given a firewall $\langle r_1, r_2, \cdots, r_n \rangle$, we calculate an effective rule set for each rule from r_1 to r_n. If the effective rule set calculated for a rule r_i is empty, then r_i is upward redundant and is removed. Now the problem is how to calculate an effective rule set for every rule in a firewall.

We use $t.rules$ to denote the set of all the rules defined by all the decision paths in a partial FDT t. For any packet p that $p \in \bigcup_{r \in t.rules} M(r)$, there is one and only one rule in $t.rules$ that p matches. We use $t(p)$ to denote the decision of the unique rule that p matches in $t.rules$.

Given a partial FDT t and a sequence of rules $\langle r_1, r_2, \cdots, r_k \rangle$ that may be not comprehensive, we say t is *equivalent* to $\langle r_1, r_2, \cdots, r_k \rangle$ iff the following two conditions hold:

i. $\bigcup_{r \in T.rules} M(r) = \bigcup_{i=1}^{k} M(r_i)$,
ii. for any packet p that $p \in \bigcup_{r \in T.rules} M(r)$, $t(p)$ is the same as the decision of the first rule that p matches in the sequence $\langle r_1, r_2, \cdots, r_k \rangle$.

For example, the partial FDT in Figure 6.3 is equivalent to the sequence of rules $\langle (F_1 \in [20, 50]) \wedge (F_2 \in [35, 65]) \rightarrow a, \quad (F_1 \in [10, 60]) \wedge (F_2 \in [15, 45]) \rightarrow d \rangle$.

An effective rule set for each rule in a firewall is calculated with the help of partial FDTs. Consider a firewall that consists of n rules $\langle r_1, r_2, \cdots, r_n \rangle$. Our upward redundancy removal algorithm first builds a partial FDT, denoted t_1, that is equivalent to the sequence $\langle r_1 \rangle$, and calculates an effective rule set, denoted E_1, of rule r_1. Then the algorithm transforms the partial FDT t_1 to another partial FDT, denoted t_2, that is equivalent to the sequence $\langle r_1, r_2 \rangle$, and during the transformation process, we calculate an

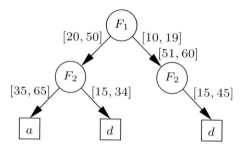

Fig. 6.3   A partial FDT

effective rule set, denoted E_2, of rule r_2. The same transformation process continues until we reach r_n. When we finish, an effective rule set is calculated for every rule.

Here we use t_i to denote the partial FDT that we constructed from the rule sequence $\langle r_1, r_2, \cdots, r_i \rangle$, and E_i to denote the effective rule set that we calculated for rule r_i. By the following example, we show the process of transforming the partial FDT t_i to the partial FDT t_{i+1}, and the calculation of E_{i+1}. Consider the firewall in Figure 6.4 over fields F_1 and F_2, where $D(F_1) = D(F_2) = [1, 100]$. Figure 6.5 shows the geometric representation of this firewall, where each rule is represented by a rectangle. From Figure 6.5, we can see that rule r_3 is upward redundant because r_3, whose area is marked by dashed lines, is totally overlaid by rules r_1 and r_2. Later we will see that the effective rule set calculated by our upward redundancy removal algorithm for rule r_3 is indeed an empty set.

$$r_1 : (F_1 \in [20, 50]) \wedge (F_2 \in [35, 65]) \rightarrow a$$
$$r_2 : (F_1 \in [10, 60]) \wedge (F_2 \in [15, 45]) \rightarrow d$$
$$r_3 : (F_1 \in [30, 40]) \wedge (F_2 \in [25, 55]) \rightarrow a$$
$$r_4 : (F_1 \in [1, 100]) \wedge (F_2 \in [1, 100]) \rightarrow d$$

Fig. 6.4   A firewall of 4 rules

Figure 6.6 shows a partial FDT t_1 that is equivalent to $\langle r_1 \rangle$ and the effective rule set E_1 calculated for rule r_1. In this figure, we use v_1 to denote the node with label F_1, e_1 to denote the edge with label $[20, 50]$, and v_2 to denote the node with label F_2.

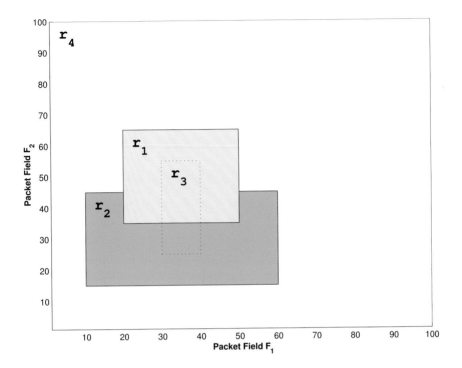

Fig. 6.5 Geometric representation of the rules in Figure 6.4

Now we show how to append rule r_2 to t_1 in order to get a partial FDT t_2 that is equivalent to $\langle r_1, r_2 \rangle$, and how to calculate an effective rule set E_2 for rule r_2. Rule r_2 is $(F_1 \in [10, 60]) \wedge (F_2 \in [15, 45]) \rightarrow d$. We first compare the set $[10, 60]$ with the set $[20, 50]$ labelled on the outgoing edge of v_1. Since $[10, 60] - [20, 50] = [10, 19] \cup [51, 60]$, r_2 is the first matching rule for all the packets that satisfy $F_1 \in [10, 19] \cup [51, 60] \wedge F_2 \in [15, 45]$, so we add one outgoing edge e to v_1, where e is labeled $[10, 19] \cup [51, 60]$ and e points to the path built from $F_2 \in [15, 45] \rightarrow d$. The rule defined by the decision path containing e, i.e., $F_1 \in [10, 19] \cup [51, 60] \wedge F_2 \in [15, 45] \rightarrow d$, should be put in E_2 because for all packets that match this rule, r_2 is their first matching rule. Since $[20, 50] \subset [10, 60]$, r_2 is possibly the first matching rule for a packet that satisfies $F_1 \in [20, 50]$. So we further compare the set $[35, 65]$ labeled on the outgoing edge of v_2 with the set $[15, 45]$. Since $[15, 45] - [35, 65] = [15, 34]$, we add a new edge e' to v_2, where e' is labeled $[15, 34]$ and e' points to a terminal node labeled d. Similarly, we

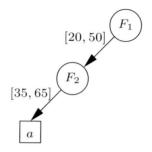

$$E_1 = \{F_1 \in [20, 50] \wedge F_2 \in [35, 65] \to a\}$$

Fig. 6.6   Partial FDT t_1 and the effective rule set E_1 calculated for rule r_1 in Figure 6.4

add the rule, $F_1 \in [20, 50] \wedge F_2 \in [15, 34] \to d$, defined by the decision path containing the new edge e' into E_2. The partial FDT t_2 and the effective rule set E_2 of rule r_2 is shown in Figure 6.7.

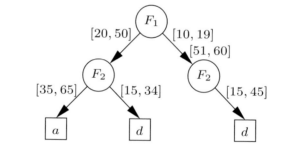

$$E_2 = \{F_1 \in [10, 19] \cup [51, 60] \wedge F_2 \in [15, 45] \to d$$
$$F_1 \in [20, 50] \wedge F_2 \in [15, 34] \qquad\qquad \to d\}$$

Fig. 6.7   Partial FDT t_2 and the effective rule set E_2 calculated for rule r_2 in Figure 6.4

Let f be any firewall that consists of n rules: $\langle r_1, r_2, \cdots, r_n \rangle$. The partial FDT that is equivalent to $\langle r_1 \rangle$ consists of only one decision path that defines the rule r_1.

Suppose that we have constructed a partial FDT t_i that is equivalent to the sequence $\langle r_1, r_2, \cdots, r_i \rangle$, and have calculated an effective rule set for each of these i rules. Let v be the root of t_i, and assume v has k outgoing edges $e_1, e_2, \cdots, e_k$. Let rule r_{i+1} be $(F_1 \in S_1) \wedge (F_2 \in S_2) \wedge$

$\cdots \wedge (F_d \in S_d) \rightarrow \langle decision \rangle$. Next we consider how to transform the partial FDT t_i to a partial FDT, denoted t_{i+1}, that is equivalent to the sequence $\langle r_1, r_2, \cdots, r_i, r_{i+1} \rangle$, and during the transformation process, how to calculate an effective rule set, denoted E_{i+1}, for rule r_{i+1}.

First, we examine whether we need to add another outgoing edge to v. If $S_1 - (I(e_1) \cup I(e_2) \cup \cdots \cup I(e_k)) \neq \emptyset$, we need to add a new outgoing edge e_{k+1} with label $S_1 - (I(e_1) \cup I(e_2) \cup \cdots \cup I(e_k))$ to v. This is because any packet, whose F_1 field satisfies $S_1 - (I(e_1) \cup I(e_2) \cup \cdots \cup I(e_k))$, does not match any of the first i rules, but matches r_{i+1} provided that the packet also satisfies $(F_2 \in S_2) \wedge (F_3 \in S_3) \wedge \cdots \wedge (F_d \in S_d)$. The new edge e_{k+1} points to the root of the path that is built from $(F_2 \in S_2) \wedge (F_3 \in S_3) \wedge \cdots \wedge (F_d \in S_d) \rightarrow \langle decision \rangle$. The rule r, $(F_1 \in S_1 - (I(e_1) \cup I(e_2) \cup \cdots \cup I(e_k))) \wedge (F_2 \in S_2) \wedge \cdots \wedge (F_d \in S_d) \rightarrow \langle decision \rangle$, defined by the decision path containing the new edge e_{k+1} has the property $M(r) \subseteq R(r_{i+1}, f)$. Therefore, we add rule r to E_i.

Second, we compare S_1 and $I(e_j)$ for each j $(1 \leq j \leq k)$ in the following three cases:

i. $S_1 \cap I(e_j) = \emptyset$: In this case, we skip edge e_j because any packet whose value of field F_1 is in set $I(e_j)$ doesn't match r_{i+1}.

ii. $S_1 \cap I(e_j) = I(e_j)$: In this case, for a packet p whose value of field F_1 is in set $I(e_j)$, the first rule that p matches may be one of the first i rules, and may be rule r_{i+1}. So we append $(F_2 \in S_2) \wedge (F_3 \in S_3) \wedge \cdots \wedge (F_d \in S_d) \rightarrow \langle decision \rangle$ to the subtree rooted at the node that e_j points to in a similar fashion.

iii. $S_1 \cap I(e_j) \neq \emptyset$ and $S_1 \cap I(e_j) \neq I(e_j)$: In this case, we split edge e into two edges: e' with label $I(e_j) - S_1$ and e'' with label $I(e_j) \cap S_1$. Then we make two copies of the subtree rooted at the node that e_j points to, and let e' and e'' point to one copy each. Thus we can deal with e' by the first case, and e'' by the second case.

In the process of appending rule r_{i+1} to partial FDT t_i, each time that we add a new edge to a node in t_i, the rule defined by the decision path containing the new edge is added to E_{i+1}. After the partial FDT t_i is transformed to t_{i+1}, according to the transformation process, the rules in E_{i+1} satisfy the following two conditions: (1) the union of all the matching sets of these rules is the resolving set of r_{i+1}, (2) all these rules have the same decision as r_{i+1}. Therefore, E_{i+1} is an effective rule set of rule r_{i+1}.

The pseudocode for removing upward redundant rules is as follows. In the algorithm, we use $e.t$ to denote the node that edge e points to.

Upward Redundancy Removal Algorithm
input : A firewall f that consists of n rules $\langle r_1, r_2 \cdots, r_n \rangle$
output: (1) Upward redundant rules in f are removed.
         (2) An effective rules set for each rule is calculated.

1. Build a decision path from rule r_1 and let v be the root;
2. **for** $i := 2$ **to** n **do**
     (1) $E_i := \emptyset$;
     (2) **Ecal**(v, i, r_i);
     (3) **if** $E_i = \emptyset$ **then** remove r_i;

Ecal(v, i, $(F_j \in S_j) \wedge \cdots \wedge (F_d \in S_d) \rightarrow \langle decision \rangle$)
/*$F(v) = F_j$ and $E(v) = \{e_1, \cdots, e_k\}$*/
1. **if** $S_j - (I(e_1) \cup \cdots \cup I(e_k)) \neq \emptyset$ **then**
     (1) Add an outgoing edge e_{k+1} with label $S_j - (I(e_1) \cup \cdots \cup I(e_k))$ to v;
     (2) Build a path from $(F_{j+1} \in S_{j+1}) \wedge \cdots \wedge (F_d \in S_d) \rightarrow \langle decision \rangle$,
         and let e_{k+1} point to its root;
     (3) Add the rule defined by the decision path containing edge e_{k+1} to E_i;
2. **if** $j < d$ **then**
     for $g := 1$ **to** k **do**
         if $I(e_g) \subseteq S_j$ **then**
             Ecal($e_g.t$, i, $(F_{j+1} \in S_{j+1}) \wedge \cdots \wedge (F_d \in S_d) \rightarrow \langle decision \rangle$);
         else if $I(e_j) \cap S_i \neq \emptyset$ **then**
             (1) $I(e_g) := I(e_g) - S_j$;
             (2) Add one outgoing edge e with label $I(e_g) \cap S_j$ to v;
             (3) Replicate the graph rooted at $e_g.t$, and
                 let e points to the replicated graph;
             (4) **Ecal**($e.t$, i, $(F_{j+1} \in S_{j+1}) \wedge \cdots \wedge (F_d \in S_d) \rightarrow \langle decision \rangle$);

By applying our upward redundancy removal algorithm to the firewall in Figure 6.4, we get an effective rule set for each rule as shown in Figure 6.8. Note that $E_3 = \emptyset$, which means that rule r_3 is upward redundant, therefore r_3 is removed.

6.3 Removing Downward Redundancy

One particular advantage of detecting and removing upward redundant rules before detecting and removing downward redundant rules in a fire-

$$1 : E_1 = \{F_1 \in [20, 50] \land F_2 \in [35, 65] \qquad \rightarrow a\};$$
$$2 : E_2 = \{F_1 \in [10, 19] \cup [51, 60] \land F_2 \in [15, 45] \quad \rightarrow d$$
$$\qquad F_1 \in [20, 50] \land F_2 \in [15, 34] \qquad \rightarrow d\};$$
$$3 : E_3 = \emptyset;$$
$$4 : E_4 = \{$$
$$\quad F_1 \in [1, 9] \cup [61, 100] \land F_2 \in [1, 100] \qquad \rightarrow d$$
$$\quad F_1 \in [20, 29] \cup [41, 50] \land F_2 \in [1, 14] \cup [66, 100] \rightarrow d$$
$$\quad F_1 \in [30, 40] \land F_2 \in [1, 14] \cup [66, 100] \qquad \rightarrow d$$
$$\quad F_1 \in [10, 19] \cup [51, 60] \land F_2 \in [1, 14] \cup [46, 100] \rightarrow d\}$$

Fig. 6.8   Effective rule sets calculated for the firewall in Figure 6.4

wall is that an effective rule set for each rule is calculated by the upward redundancy removal algorithm; therefore, we can use the effective rule set of a rule to check whether the rule is downward redundant. Note that knowing an effective rule set of a rule equals knowing the resolving set of the rule.

Our algorithm for removing downward redundant rules is based on the following theorem.

Theorem 6.3.1. Let f be any firewall that consists of n rules: $\langle r_1, r_2, \cdots, r_n \rangle$. Let t'_i ($2 \leq i \leq n$) be an FDT that is equivalent to the sequence of rules $\langle r_i, r_{i+1}, \cdots, r_n \rangle$. The rule r_{i-1} with the effective rule set E_{i-1} is downward redundant in f iff for each rule r in E_{i-1} and for each decision path $(v_1 e_1 v_2 e_2 \cdots v_d e_d v_{d+1})$ in t'_i where rule r overlaps the rule that is defined by this decision path, the decision of r is the same as the label of the terminal node v_{d+1}.

Proof Sketch: Since the sequence of rules $\langle r_i, r_{i+1}, \cdots, r_n \rangle$ is comprehensive, there exists an FDT that is equivalent to this sequence of rules. By the redundancy theorem, rule r_{i-1} is downward redundant iff for each rule r in E_{i-1} and for any p that $p \in M(r)$, $\langle r_i, r_{i+1}, \cdots, r_n \rangle (p)$ is the same as the decision of r. Therefore, Theorem 6.3.1 follows.   □

Now we consider how to construct an FDT t'_i, $2 \leq i \leq n$, that is equivalent to the sequence of rules $\langle r_i, r_{i+1}, \cdots, r_n \rangle$. The FDT t'_n can be built from rule r_n in the same way that we build a path from a rule in the upward redundancy removal algorithm.

Suppose we have constructed an FDT t'_i that is equivalent to the sequence of rules $\langle r_i, r_{i+1}, \cdots, r_n \rangle$. First, we check whether rule r_{i-1} is downward redundant by Theorem 6.3.1. If rule r_{i-1} is downward redundant, then we remove r_i, rename the FDT t'_i to be t'_{i-1}, and continue to check whether r_{i-2} is downward redundant. If rule r_{i-1} is not downward redundant, then we append rule r_{i-1} to the FDT t'_i such that the resulting tree is an FDT, denoted t'_{i-1}, that is equivalent to the sequence of rules $\langle r_{i-1}, r_i, \cdots, r_n \rangle$. This procedure of transforming an FDT by appending a rule is similar to the procedure of transforming a partial FDT in the upward redundancy removal algorithm. The above process continues until we reach r_1; therefore, all downward redundant rules are detected and removed.

The pseudocode for detecting and removing downward redundant rules is as follows.

Downward Redundancy Removal Algorithm
input : A firewall $\langle r_1, r_2 \cdots, r_n \rangle$ where each rule r_i has an effective rule set E_i.
output: Downward redundant rules in f are removed.

1. Build a decision path from rule r_n and let v be the root;
2. **for** $i := n - 1$ **to** 1 **do**
      if IsDownwardRedundant(v, E_i) = *true*
      then remove r_i;
      else Append(v, r_i);

IsDownwardRedundant(v, E) /*$E = \{r'_1, \cdots, r'_m\}$*/
1. **for** $j := 1$ **to** m **do**
      if HaveSameDecision(v, r'_j) = *false* **then**
          return(*false*);
2. **return**(*true*);

HaveSameDecision(v, $(F_i \in S_i) \wedge \cdots \wedge (F_d \in S_d) \rightarrow \langle decision \rangle$)
/*$F(v) = F_i$ and $E(v) = \{e_1, \cdots, e_k\}$*/
1. **for** $j := 1$ **to** k **do**
      if $I(e_j) \cap S_i \neq \emptyset$ **then**
          if $i < d$ **then**
              if HaveSameDecision$(e_j.t, (F_{i+1} \in S_{i+1})$
                  $\wedge \cdots \wedge (F_d \in S_d) \rightarrow \langle decision \rangle$) = **false**
              then return(*false*);
          else
              if $F(e_j.t) \neq \langle decision \rangle$ **then return**(*false*);

2. **return**(*true*);

Append(v, $(F_i \in S_i) \wedge \cdots \wedge (F_d \in S_d) \to \langle decision \rangle$)
/*$F(v) = F_i$ and $E(v) = \{e_1, \cdots, e_k\}$*/
if $i < d$ **then**
   for $j := 1$ **to** k **do**
     if $I(e_j) \subseteq S_i$ **then**
       Append($e_j.t$, $(F_{i+1} \in S_{i+1}) \wedge \cdots \wedge (F_d \in S_d) \to \langle decision \rangle$);
     else if $I(e_j) \cap S_i \neq \emptyset$ **then**
        (1) $I(e_j) := I(e_j) - S_i$;
        (2) Add one outgoing edge e with label $I(e_j) \cap S_i$ to v;
        (3) Replicate the graph rooted at $e_j.t$, and
           let e points to the replicated graph;
        (4) **Append**($e.t$, $(F_{i+1} \in S_{i+1}) \wedge \cdots \wedge (F_d \in S_d) \to \langle decision \rangle$);
else /*$i = d$*/
   (1) **for** $j := 1$ **to** k **do**
     (a) $I(e_j) := I(e_j) - S_i$;
     (b) **if** $I(e_j) = \emptyset$ **then** remove edge e_i and node $e_i.t$;
   (2) Add one outgoing edge e with label S_i to v,
     create a terminal node with label $\langle decision \rangle$,
     and let e point this terminal node;

Applying our downward redundancy removal algorithm to the firewall in Figure 6.4, assuming r_3 has been removed, rule r_2 is detected to be downward redundant, therefore r_2 is removed. The FDT in Figure 6.9 is the resulting FDT by appending rule r_1 to the FDT that is equivalent to $\langle r_4 \rangle$.

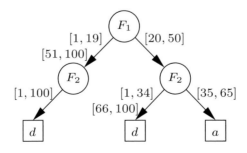

Fig. 6.9   An FDT

The time and space complexity of the upward and downward redundancy removal algorithm is $O(n^d)$, where n is the total number of rules and d is the total number of distinct packet fields that are examined by a firewall. Although in the worst case our algorithms need n^d time and space, our algorithms are practical for two reasons. First, d is typically small. Most real-life firewalls only examine four packet fields: source IP address, destination IP address, destination port number and protocol type. Second, the worst case of our algorithms are very unlikely to happen in real-life.

6.4   Experimental Results

In this section, we evaluate the efficiency of the upward and downward redundancy removal algorithms. In the absence of publicly available firewalls, we create synthetic firewalls that embody the important characteristics of real-life firewalls that have been discovered so far in [Gupta (2000)].

We implemented the algorithms in this chapter in SUN Java JDK 1.4 [Java (2004)]. The experiments were carried out on one SunBlade 2000 machine running Solaris 9 with a 1Ghz CPU and 1 GB of memory. The average processing time for removing all upward and downward redundant rules from a firewall versus the total number of rules in the firewall is shown in Figure 6.10. From this figure, we can see that the running time of our algorithms increases slightly faster than linearly as the number of rules grows. This shows that our redundancy removal algorithms are efficient enough for practical uses. For example, it takes less than 3 seconds to remove all the redundant rules from a firewall that has up to 3000 rules, and it takes less than 6 seconds to remove all the redundant rules from a firewall that has up to 6000 rules. In fact, most real-life firewalls have less than 1000 rules [Gupta (2000)].

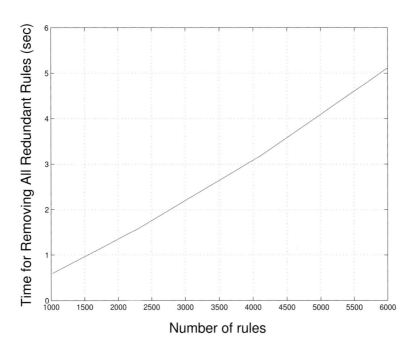

Fig. 6.10   Average processing time for removing all (both upward and downward) redundant rules vs. Total number of rules in a firewall

Chapter 7

Epilogue

7.1 Conclusions

Towards the goal of correct firewalls, in this book, we rigorously and systematically studied the two fundamental problems of how to design a new firewall such that the errors introduced in the design phase is reduced and how to analyze an existing firewall such that the errors that have been built-in in the design phase can be detected.

In this book, we made the following five major contributions:

i. We presented the method of structured firewall design. This design method addresses all the three problems of consistency, completeness and compactness in designing firewalls. Using this design method, a firewall administrator only needs to focus on the high-level logical design of a firewall. A series of five algorithms can automatically convert the high-level logical design into low-level firewall rules.

ii. We presented the method of diverse firewall design. This method can greatly reduce the human errors introduced in the design phase. This method is the first attempt of applying the principle of diverse design to firewalls. The method for comparing two given firewalls could be used for many other purposes such as change-impact analysis.

iii. We presented a model for specifying stateful firewalls. This model can express a variety of state tracking functionalities. It also allows us to inherit the rich results in stateless firewall design and analysis. Furthermore, it provides backward compatibility such that a stateless firewall can also be specified using our model.

iv. We presented a method of querying firewalls, which includes a language for specifying firewall queries and an algorithm for processing firewall queries. This method is very helpful for firewall administrators to debug and non-intrusively test existing firewalls.

v. We presented a method of detecting redundant rules in a firewall. This is the first algorithm that can detect all the redundant rules in a firewall, which means that the resulting firewall after all the redundant rules are removed has no redundant rules. Detecting redundant rules is useful in detecting firewall errors because a rule being redundant may not be the intent of the firewall administrator. Removing useless redundant rules improves the performance of firewalls.

The design and analysis methods presented in this book are not limited to firewalls. Rather, they are extensible to other rule-based systems such as general packet classification systems and IPsec. This extension is fairly straightforward.

Acknowledgments

The firewall design and analysis methods in this book were developed in my Ph.D. studies under the supervision of Professor Mohamed Gouda. His taste in research topics, his rigor of thinking, his clarity of purpose, his insistence on elegance, and his high standard of excellence have shaped the substance of this book. I am always grateful for his invaluable advice and support during my graduate studies.

Bibliography

Al-Shaer, E. and Hamed, H. (2003a). Firewall policy advisor for anomaly detection and rule editing, in *IEEE/IFIP Integrated Management IM'2003*, pp. 17–30.

Al-Shaer, E. and Hamed, H. (2003b). Management and translation of filtering security policies, in *IEEE International Conference on Communications*, pp. 256–260, URL http://www.mnlab.cs.depaul.edu/~ehab/papers/ICC03-fw.pdf.

Al-Shaer, E. and Hamed, H. (2004). Discovery of policy anomalies in distributed firewalls, in *IEEE INFOCOM'04*, pp. 2605–2616.

Anderson, H. and Hagelin, G. (1981). Computer controlled interlocking system, *Ericsson Review* , 2.

Avizienis, A. (1985). The n-version approach to fault tolerant software, *IEEE Transactions on Software Engineering* **SE-11**, 12, pp. 1491–1501.

Avizienis, A. (1995). The methodology of n-version programming, *Chapter 2 of Software Fault Tolerance, M. R. Lyu (ed.), Wiley, 23-46* URL citeseer.nj.nec.com/avizienis95methodology.html.

Avizienis, A. and Chen, L. (1977). On the implementation of n-version programming for software fault-tolerance during program execution, in *Proceedings of Intl. Computer software and Appl. Conf.*, pp. 145–155.

Baboescu, F., Singh, S. and Varghese, G. (2003). Packet classification for core routers: Is there an alternative to cams? in *Proceedings of IEEE INFOCOM*.

Baboescu, F. and Varghese, G. (2001). Scalable packet classification, in *Proceedings of ACM SIGCOMM*, pp. 199–210, URL http://citeseer.nj.nec.com/baboescu01scalable.html.

Baboescu, F. and Varghese, G. (2002). Fast and scalable conflict detection for packet classifiers, in *Proceedings of the 10th IEEE International Conference on Network Protocols*, URL citeseer.nj.nec.com/583775.html.

Bartal, Y., Mayer, A. J., Nissim, K. and Wool, A. (1999). Firmato: A novel firewall management toolkit, in *Proceeding of the IEEE Symposium on Security and Privacy*, pp. 17–31, URL citeseer.ist.psu.edu/bartal99firmato.html.

Bartal, Y., Mayer, A. J., Nissim, K. and Wool, A. (2003). Firmato: A novel firewall management toolkit, *Technical Report EES2003-1, Dept. of Electrical Engineering Systems, Tel Aviv University* .

Begel, A., McCanne, S. and Graham, S. L. (1999). BPF+: Exploiting global dataflow optimization in a generalized packet filter architecture, in *Proceedings of ACM SIGCOMM '99*, URL `citeseer.nj.nec.com/begel99bpf.html`.

Bryant, R. E. (1986). Graph-based algorithms for boolean function manipulation, *IEEE Trans. on Computers* **35**, 8, pp. 677–691, URL `citeseer.nj.nec.com/bryant86graphbased.html`.

Condor, A. and Hinton, G. (1988). Fault tolerant and fail-safe design of candu computerised shutdown systems, *IAEA Specialist Meeting on Microprocessors important to the Safety of Nuclear Power Plants,* .

Dijkstra, E. W. (1968). Goto statement considered harmful, *Communications of the ACM* **11**, 3, pp. 147–148.

Eppstein, D. and Muthukrishnan, S. (2001). Internet packet filter management and rectangle geometry, in *Symp. on Discrete Algorithms*, pp. 827–835, URL `citeseer.nj.nec.com/eppstein01internet.html`.

Eronen, P. and Zitting, J. (2001). An expert system for analyzing firewall rules, in *Proceedings of the 6th Nordic Workshop on Secure IT Systems (NordSec 2001)*, pp. 100–107, URL `citeseer.nj.nec.com/eronen01expert.html`.

Farmer, D. and Venema, W. (1993). Improving the security of your site by breaking into it, *http://www.alw.nih.gov/Security/Docs/admin-guide-to-cracking.101.html* .

Frantzen, M., Kerschbaum, F., Schultz, E. and Fahmy, S. (2001). A framework for understanding vulnerabilities in firewalls using a dataflow model of firewall internals, *Computers and Security* **20**, 3, pp. 263–270.

Freiss, M. (1998). *Protecting Networks with SATAN* (O'Reilly & Associates, Inc.).

Gouda, M. G. and Liu, A. X. (2004). Firewall design: consistency, completeness and compactness, in *Proceedings of the 24th IEEE International Conference on Distributed Computing Systems (ICDCS-04)*, pp. 320–327, URL `http://www.cs.utexas.edu/users/alex/publications/fdd.pdf`.

Gouda, M. G. and Liu, A. X. (2005). A model of stateful firewalls and its properties, in *Proceedings of the IEEE International Conference on Dependable Systems and Networks (DSN-05)*, pp. 320–327, URL `http://www.cs.utexas.edu/users/alex/publications/Stateful/stateful.pdf`.

Gupta, P. (2000). *Algorithms for Routing Lookups and Packet Classification*, Ph.D. thesis, Stanford University.

Gupta, P. and McKeown, N. (2001). Algorithms for packet classification, *IEEE Network* **15**, 2, pp. 24–32, URL `citeseer.nj.nec.com/article/gupta01algorithms.html`.

Guttman, J. D. (1997). Filtering postures: Local enforcement for global policies, in *Proceedings of IEEE Symp. on Security and Privacy*, pp. 120–129, URL `citeseer.nj.nec.com/guttman97filtering.html`.

Hari, A., Suri, S. and Parulkar, G. M. (2000). Detecting and resolving packet filter conflicts, in *Proceedings of IEEE INFOCOM*, pp. 1203–1212, URL `citeseer.nj.nec.com/hari00detecting.html`.

Hazelhurst, S., Attar, A. and Sinnappan, R. (2000). Algorithms for improving the dependability of firewall and filter rule lists, in *Proceedings of the Workshop on Dependability of IP Applications, Platforms and Networks*.

Java (2004). http://java.sun.com/, .

Kamara, S., Fahmy, S., Schultz, E., Kerschbaum, F. and Frantzen, M. (2003). Analysis of vulnerabilities in internet firewalls, *Computers and Security* **22**, 3, pp. 214–232.

Liu, A. X. and Gouda, M. G. (2004). Diverse firewall design, in *Proceedings of the International Conference on Dependable Systems and Networks (DSN-04)*, pp. 595–604.

Liu, A. X. and Gouda, M. G. (2005). Complete redundancy detection in firewalls, in *Proceedings of 19th Annual IFIP Conference on Data and Applications Security, LNCS 3654, S. Jajodia and D. Wijesekera Ed., Springer-Verlag*, pp. 196–209, URL http://www.cs.utexas.edu/users/alex/publications/Redundancy/redundancy.pdf.

Liu, A. X., Gouda, M. G., Ma, H. H. and Ngu, A. H. (2004). Firewall queries, in *Proceedings of the 8th International Conference on Principles of Distributed Systems, LNCS 3544, T. Higashino Ed., Springer-Verlag*, pp. 124–139, URL http://www.cs.utexas.edu/users/alex/publications/query.pdf.

Mayer, A., Wool, A. and Ziskind, E. (2000). Fang: A firewall analysis engine, in *Proceedings of IEEE Symp. on Security and Privacy*, pp. 177–187.

Moffett, J. D. and Sloman, M. S. (1994). Policy conflict analysis in distributed system management, *Journal of Organizational Computing* **4**, 1, pp. 1–22.

Nessus (2004). http://www.nessus.org/, .

Postel, J. (1981). Internet control message protocol. *RFC 792* .

Postel, J. and Reynolds, J. (1985). File transfer protocol, *RFC 959* .

Qiu, L., Varghese, G. and Suri, S. (2001). Fast firewall implementations for software-based and hardware-based routers, in *Proceedings the 9th International Conference on Network Protocols (ICNP)*, URL citeseer.nj.nec.com/qiu01fast.html.

Quinlan, J. (1986). Induction of decision trees, *Machine Learning* **1**, 1, pp. 81–106.

Singh, S., Baboescu, F., Varghese, G. and Wang, J. (2003). Packet classification using multidimensional cutting, in *Proceedings of ACM SIGCOMM*.

Spitznagel, E., Taylor, D. and Turner, J. (2003). Packet classification using extended tcams, in *Proceedings of IEEE International Conference on Network Protocols (ICNP)*.

Srinivasan, V., Suri, S. and Varghese, G. (1999). Packet classification using tuple space search, in *Proceedings of ACM SIGCOMM*, pp. 135–146, URL citeseer.nj.nec.com/srinivasan99packet.html.

Srinivasan, V., Varghese, G., Suri, S. and Waldvogel, M. (1998). Fast and scalable layer four switching, in *Proceedings of ACM SIGCOMM*, pp. 191–202, URL citeseer.nj.nec.com/srinivasan98fast.html.

Strehl, K. and Thiele, L. (2000). Interval diagrams for efficient symbolic verification of process networks, *IEEE Trans. on Computer-Aided Design of Integrated Circuits and Systems* **19**, 8, pp. 939–956, URL http://www.tik.

`ee.ethz.ch/~tec/WWW_old_user/strehl/English/Publications.htm`.

Teng, X. and Pham, H. (2002). A software-reliability growth model for n-version programming systems, *IEEE Transactions on Reliability* **51**, 3, pp. 311–321.

Traverse, P. (1988). Airbus and atr system architecture and specification, *Software Diversity in Computerised Control Systems, U. Voges (ed.), Springer Verlag*
.

Vouk, M. A. (1988a). On back-to-back testing, in *Proceedings of Annual Conference on Computer Assurance (COMPASS)*, pp. 84–91.

Vouk, M. A. (1988b). On growing software reliability using back-to-back testing, in *Proceedings 11th Minnowbrook Workshop on Software Reliability*.

Woo, T. Y. C. (2000). A modular approach to packet classification: Algorithms and results, in *Proceedings of IEEE INFOCOM*, pp. 1213–1222, URL `citeseer.nj.nec.com/woo00modular.html`.

Wool, A. (2001). Architecting the lumeta firewall analyzer, in *Proceedings of the 10th USENIX Security Symposium*, pp. 85–97.

Wool, A. (2004). A quantitative study of firewall configuration errors, *IEEE Computer* **37**, 6, pp. 62–67.

Index